W9-BRI-745

Child's Play

First edition for the United States, its territories and dependencies, and Canada published in 2009
by Barron's Educational Series.

Conceived and produced by

Elwin Street Productions

144 Liverpool Road

London N1 1LA

United Kingdom

www.elwinstreet.com

All inquiries should be addressed to:

Barron's Educational Series

250 Wireless Boulevard

Hauppauge, NY 11788

www.barronseduc.com

ISBN-13: 978-0-7641-4241-3
ISBN-10: 0-7641-4241-0

Library of Congress Control Number: 2008937167

Designer: James Lawrence

Illustrator: Isabel Alberdi

Printed in China

10 9 8 7 6 5 4 3 2 1

The activities described in this book are to be carried out with parental supervision at all times.
Every effort has been made by to ensure the safety of activities detailed. Neither the author nor
the publishers shall be liable or responsible for any harm or damage done allegedly arising from
any information or suggestion in this book. *Child's Play* has been written by a qualified
Montessori teacher but is not approved, endorsed or affiliated with Montessori in any way.

PICTURE CREDITS
The publishers would like to thank the following for permission to reproduce images
Photolibrary: Front cover; DK Images: pp 10, 76; Paul Bricknell: pp 30, 48, 110;
Getty Images: p 128.

Child's Play

Montessori games and activities
for your baby and toddler

Maja Pitamic
Expert Contributor: Dr. Claire McCarthy

BARRON'S

Contents

Chapter 4 GAMES AND MOVEMENT

Chapter 5 LANGUAGE AND STORIES

Chapter 6 OUT AND ABOUT

Templates

Index

Introduction by Dr. Claire McCarthy

As a pediatrician, and as a mom raising five children, I can honestly say that playing isn't just fun—it's one of the best things you can do with your child. First and foremost, playing tells your child that she is important to you, that spending time with her is a priority. It gives you a chance to get to know your child better, and to make your relationship with her richer and more fulfilling. With every hug, every laugh, every tea party or game of hide-and-seek, you are creating the warm memories of childhood and building a happy, confident person.

Playing is also how children learn. This book offers ideas for games and activities for small children that are not only wonderfully educational, but fun and nurturing in the very best ways. Through jumping, climbing, and other action games they learn how to use their bodies. Through playing with blocks, play dough, or making necklaces with pasta they learn to use their hands. They learn about colors and shapes through art projects, about language from telling stories, about the world through walks in the park or trips to the zoo. They learn to share and make friends by playing with other children. And every time a child plays, there is the chance to use and stretch the imagination.

The first few years of a child's life are crucial for intellectual and emotional development. The brain is growing at a rapid rate, and the experiences of the child can actually shape the way it grows. The interactions children experience, the ways that they are loved and nurtured, fundamentally influence how they will see the world and feel about themselves for the rest of their lives.

So play. Play every day. Use the games in this book and make up games of your own. Be creative—but don't worry about making it perfect. Just have fun together, and everything else will follow.

How to use this book

This book provides activities for you to play with your child and is aimed at children aged between one and three years. Each chapter contains activities aimed at this age range. The activities are based on Montessori principles of learning through experience, but rest assured there is no need to create a Montessori classroom in your own home. They require little preparation and use readily available materials. Do not worry if you have no specialist knowledge of teaching. The points below will guide you through the essential steps when presenting an activity for your child.

■ All the activities are suitable for boys and girls. To avoid repetition, the use of "she" and "he" is alternated in the chapters.

■ Each chapter opens with a timeline, marking key milestones in your child's development. These are meant as a rough guide only, children develop at their own pace, some will grasp new skills faster than others.

■ Check your environment. Make sure that you and your child can do the activity in comfort and safety.

■ Make sure that your child can see the activity clearly. Sit your child to the left of you (to your right, if she is left-handed). Aim to work with your right hand (your left hand, if your child is left-handed) for consistency.

■ Prepare the activity in advance. There is no point suggesting an activity to a child only to discover that you don't have the materials.

■ Be clear in your own mind what the aim of the activity is; always read it through first.

■ Try not to be negative. If your child is unable to do the activity correctly, then make a mental note to reintroduce it again at a later stage.

■ If your child abuses any of the materials in the activity, then the activity needs to be removed immediately. By doing this, she will understand that her behavior was unacceptable. The activity can be reintroduced at a later date.

■ While a structured approach is needed, be prepared to be flexible and don't worry if things don't always go as planned; it may lead your child down unexpected paths of discovery, and that's when things get exciting.

Development through play

As adults, we often underestimate the value that play has in developing children both mentally and physically. Play is your child's way of engaging and making sense of the world and cannot be overvalued. Take an activity like role-play. This may appear to be a very simple activity, yet within it, young children can learn the practical life skills of dressing, setting the table, and how to cooperate and share with others.

For adults the sense of sight is the dominant sense, but for very young children all their senses are heightened. A child's senses are her natural teaching tools for exploring her world. The games and activities contained in this book engage all the senses to develop your child's co-ordination, concentration, and life skills. They will also help to relieve your child's sense of frustration, which is a key characteristic of this age group. Your child will be engaged both mentally and physically to gain a sense of independence and self-worth.

Montessori teaching principles

The games and activities in this book require no specialist knowledge or equipment. They are based on key Montessori principles of learning through experience. Maria Montessori was born in Rome in 1870. She was the first female medical graduate of Rome University, became the director of the Scuola Ortofrenica, a school for children with special education needs, and by 1900, she was teaching Pedagogical Anthropology at Rome University. In 1907, Montessori opened the first Casa dei Bambini, a school for children from slums. While there, she devised her now world-famous teaching method. Word spread quickly of the revolutionary teaching method that was being employed in the schools, and soon visitors were flocking to observe. The Montessori teaching method became internationally renowned.

Possibly Montessori's most revolutionary belief was the importance of the child's environment when learning. She felt that for children to flourish and grow in self-esteem, they needed to work in a child-centered environment. Today, not only Montessori schools, but all schools recognize the part that the environment has to play in the development of the child.

Montessori always claimed that she did not devise a teaching method but that her ideas on teaching children merely grew out of close observation of children. From this, she discovered that children need to have joy in learning, a love of order, and an interest in fact and fiction, as well as to be independent and to be respected and listened to.

This book presents my interpretation of Montessori drawn from my years of teaching. The activities follow the spirit, rather than the letter, of Montessori. They come with a list of any items you will need to complete the activity, simple step-by-step instructions, and further extension activities that will continue to challenge your child as she grows in confidence and age and becomes able to tackle more complex activities with you. Not only will your child be on a path of discovery, but you too will discover what excites, stimulates, or frustrates her—and you! But best of all, you will be able to share her sense of accomplishment when she masters a new skill.

Exploring senses

In the adult world it is the sense of sight that dominates above all the other senses, and it is very easy to forget just what a key role all the senses have in the development of the young child. For young children the senses are their natural tools of learning. Think how a baby will want to explore new objects orally or how a toddler's fingers will constantly be moving over surfaces. It's their way of investigating and discovering the world around them. In the following chapter, you will find a variety of activities that will introduce and explore all the senses.

Development timeline: 1–1½ years

Between the ages of twelve and eighteen months, your child will be able to do more and more for himself. By the time he reaches his first birthday, he should be able to stand up on his own and should now be beginning to walk without support. He will be able to transfer small objects from himself to another person by using the thumb and one finger. Attempts at communication have begun in earnest, and your child will begin to try out conversation, having mastered two or three words. He can nod to signal yes and responds to his own name.

Your child's understanding will have increased to the extent that he now knows who that person is staring back at him in the mirror. Stronger preferences for people and toys are developing, and he is imitating people during play. At this stage he favors the person who looks after him most above all others.

Having completed his graduation from liquid to solid food, he will start to be able

Timeline

| walks without support | | uses four or five words | | some self-feeding with utensils |

12 months   responds to simple requests   able to place objects in containers and take them out   **15 months**

to feed himself with a spoon, and should be well able to drink from a cup. When he speaks he is comfortable using four or five words; as he approaches eighteen months old this may be increasing to sentences of five to ten words.

By eighteen months your child's developments in strength, stability, and coordination mean that he can now pull toys with wheels, as well as being able to place objects into containers and then take them out again. The very beginnings of artistic endeavor are witnessed for the first time as he can use crayons to make a mark on paper. His spoken vocabulary has increased to as many as ten words, and he can understand easy directions given to him, such as "eat your food."

This chapter seeks to maximize your child's early sensory abilities. At this young age he will be excited to learn, even though he doesn't yet have the vocabulary, and the importance of familiarizing him with the textures, shapes, and sounds around him cannot be underestimated. So you can help your child explore and develop his senses with the activities in this chapter as he discovers the idea of objects disappearing and reappearing in Hide-and-Seek, explores textures in the Sensory Walk, and learns to associate objects with sounds in the Guess the Sound game.

uses five to
ten words

marks paper
with crayons

pulls toys on
wheels

18 months

Hide-and-seek

1+ years

The time-honored game of hiding things and revealing them again—be it faces or other objects—will keep your child almost endlessly amused. It's also an important early bonding and learning activity, simultaneously introducing the concepts of things disappearing and reappearing. Your child will begin to understand that just because she can't see something doesn't mean it isn't there.

1 Engage your child's attention, then hide your face behind your hands or a cloth.

2 Ask her where you've gone—this is important to engage her active curiosity.

3 Reveal yourself with a touch of drama—"Peekaboo!" always works well.

4 Vary the time delay, facial expressions, and accompanying noises to maintain the element of surprise, which encourages learning.

You will need

- Just your hands, or a small cloth

Other activity to try

You could hide behind furniture or try hiding a favorite toy and revealing it.

Tip box ■ Don't forget to let older children reverse the roles and try themselves. For younger children, you can hide and reveal their faces for them.

Mirror fun

1+
years

Mirrors are an endlessly useful tool in child's play—they double the fun and the learning possibilities. This mirror activity and its variations help to build vocabulary and communication skills, as well as concepts of self-awareness, which are invaluable for your child's development.

1 Settle on the floor with your child in your lap, making sure you are both clearly reflected in the mirror. You can also lay the mirror flat on the floor and look into it from above.

2 Start a question and answer routine, using the mirror. "What's this?" "It's your nose." "Where's your nose?" "There's your nose!"

3 Continue with the routine, covering all parts of the face. You can then move on to expressions, such as sad, happy, angry, tired, or silly.

4 Let the game develop as long as your child stays interested by your actions.

You will need

- Good-sized mirror
- Scarf (optional)
- Favorite toys (optional)

Other activities to try

Try hanging up a small mirror on some string so that it can spin around—your child will be able to see the reflections from different angles, as well as the different light reflections.

Use a scarf to play peekaboo (see page 14)—your child will be even more engaged when it's herself she's looking at.

You can do any number of actions and get your child to copy you; such as pointing, grabbing, or lifting.

The wacky races

All toddlers with toy cars enjoy racing them across every surface in the house. It's their way of discovering different textures. Taking my inspiration from this, the next activity recreates a miniature multi-surface racetrack using whatever materials you have to hand.

You will need

- Large tray or baking tray
- Silver foil to line the tray
- Marker
- Medium-sized ball of play dough (see page 64 for recipe) or clay
- Selection of materials for the racetrack, all with different textures. Here are some possible materials you may like to use (you can, of course, try some of your own): crushed eggshells, egg boxes, sand, shells, corrugated cardboard, marbles, buttons, pieces of bark, twigs
- A few toy cars

Tip box   ■ Do make sure you have enough materials before you start the project.

SAFETY POINT ⚠ Avoid materials that could be a potential choking or blocked nasal hazard.

1 Line the tray with the silver foil.

2 With the marker pen, mark out a windy wacky racetrack with lots of hairpin bends.

3 Take the play dough and roll it into long thin "snakes." If he is able, invite your child to help you with this.

4 Line the snakes on the foil so they follow the line of the marked racetrack. This will act as a barrier and contain the material.

5 Choose a material and fill in a section of racetrack. The area each material covers will depend upon how many materials you have. For the activity to be really effective, you should have as many materials as possible. I would suggest a minimum of four.

6 Continue sectioning the racetrack until it is complete. It is now ready for racing.

7 Give your child a collection of toy cars and let him run them around the racetrack, so that he can feel the differences between all the surfaces that you have laid on the track.

Other activities to try

You may wish to upgrade your racetrack with some of these suggestions.

Take small twigs with fir needles or leaves on and stick them into the play dough to line the racetrack with trees.

You could make road signs with pieces of paper and lollipop sticks and again stick them into the play dough.

Add miniature houses or other buildings to line the side of the track.

Guess the sound game

1+ years

Try this experiment: stop and count how many different sounds you hear in one day. I think you will be very surprised at the total. Many of these sounds you will have blanked out, for your brain has understood and recognized them. But for a child the majority of these sounds will be unknowns that need to be identified. So hearing is a sensory tool in helping children build up a greater understanding of the world around them.

This fun game will help children in building up their knowledge of different sounds, while the later activities will encourage them to identify these sounds and refine their hearing abilities.

1 Ask your child to sit on your left with the tray in front of you. Place the objects on the tray.

2 Tell your child, "We are going to play guess the sound." Point to and name aloud all of the objects on the tray.

You will need

- Tray
- 3 objects that make distinguishing sounds from one another (for example, metal or wooden spoons knocked together, a shaken packet of cereal) and which your child is familiar with
- Cloth, like a tea towel, big enough to cover the tray

Tip box

■ I would not suggest that you use musical instruments in this project as they could distract from the game.

■ Tell your child to take time to really listen to the sound before making his guess.

Other activities to try

As your child becomes more confident, add extra objects, to a maximum of six, and start to introduce new objects with unfamiliar sounds.

As he grows older and more familiar with the objects and their names, ask him to try and guess which object he thinks made that noise.

For three-year-olds, once they have mastered the game, keep the cloth on the tray. If they get stuck, verbally name with them the objects and this should give them a clue.

3 Cover the tray with the cloth. Select an object under the cloth, for example, the two spoons. Knock these together, asking your child to listen to the sound.

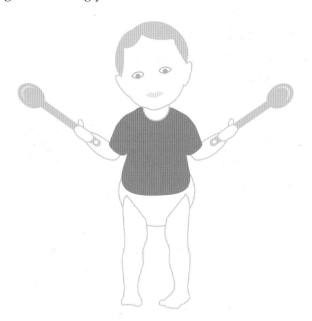

4 Remove the cloth and say out loud what object it was, then pick it up to show to your child.

5 Invite your child to make the same sound so that he can clearly see which object makes that sound. Repeat with all of the objects on the tray.

Sensory walk

1½+ years

Everyone enjoys the sensation of walking on grass with bare feet, and for young children this pleasure is doubled because they have a heightened sense of touch. In this next activity a sensory trail of different textures is laid out for your child to explore and develop her sense of touch. It also has the advantage of developing balancing skills.

You will need

- •Large indoor or outdoor space
- Variety of surfaces with different textures, e.g.:
- • 4 cushions of any size (if possible, choose cushions with different fabrics)
- • Carpet samples (from your local carpet store)
- • Small rug
- • Doormat (make sure it's not rough)
- • Large sheet of bubble wrap

1 Lay a straight path with your chosen items, each of which should have a different texture.

2 Demonstrate to your child how you would like her to walk the path, with arms out to help her balance.

3 Let your child try.

4 She will need your support at first, so begin by holding each hand. When she is more confident with this activity, let her try a few steps by herself, but be close by in case you need to steady her again.

5 Walking over the cushions will be the trickiest part, so a steadying hand from you will be required for this.

Other activities to try

After your child has mastered the path, change the order of the surfaces and introduce some new ones.

Progress from a straight path to a wavy one.

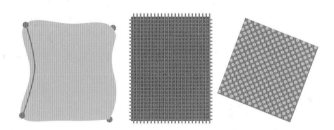

Tip box ■ Let your child repeat the path walk as many times as she wishes.

Touch and texture game

Of all the senses the sense of touch is the most predominant in children under three. With their hands outstretched, through their fingertips they explore a variety of textures. As time goes on, they begin to associate different textures with people, places, and times of the day. The soft fluffy blanket they have means security at bedtime, while the smooth shiny plastic raincoat means it's raining. This is a very adaptable game that can be graduated to suit all ages, starting with simple sorting of textural opposites to the more sophisticated textural grading.

You will need

- Container or basket big enough to put the objects in
- 6–8 small objects that are hard or soft (for example, wood, play dough, plastic, or fabric)

1 With the basket in front of you and your child to your left, take a hard object out of the basket. Put it on the left. Then take out a soft object, and put it on the right.

2 Press your fingertips into the hard object and say the word "hard." Repeat the action with the soft object and say the word "soft."

3 Pass the two objects over to your child, and invite her to feel the surfaces, as you did.

4 As she holds each object, say the words "hard" and "soft" again. Younger children will not be able to name these textures at first, but as they continue to play the game, the words will become more familiar.

5 Invite your child to sort the rest of the objects into hard or soft.

Other activities to try

Try using objects with different textural opposites like rough and smooth.

Choose objects with contrasting temperatures, like cork, wool, marble, wood, and stone. Show your child how to sort objects by temperature: warm and cold.

Graduate from two groups to three groups for sorting.

As your child gains in confidence, she might like to try the activity with her eyes closed or wearing a blindfold, but remember you will need to show her first.

A great source of objects can be found in your own garden or local park, with crisp autumn leaves, knobbly pinecones, and gnarled pieces of bark to name but a few.

Tip box
■ Choose contrasting objects so your child can clearly feel the difference between hard and soft.

■ Don't be alarmed if your child does not pick up on the language right away. Younger children in particular take time to absorb new language.

Guess the fruit or vegetable

This activity is designed to help your child develop her sense of touch by exploring the shape and textures of different fruits and vegetables. At the same time she will extend her knowledge of fruits and vegetables.

1 Explain to your child that you are going to show her how to play guess the fruit or vegetable.

2 Ask her to help carry the fruits and vegetables to the activity area. This could be the floor or a low table.

3 Place the fruits and vegetables in the center of the activity area, along with the eye mask.

4 Go through with your child the names of the fruits or vegetables that have been selected.

5 Demonstrate to your child how to put on the eye mask.

You will need

- 3 pieces of a fruit or vegetable, all different in size, shape, and texture; for example, an apple, a banana, a potato
- Eye mask or scarf

Tip box   ■ If your child is having difficulty identifying the fruit or vegetable say the name out loud. This should help but give her plenty of time before stepping in.

■ Remember that this is a sensory activity, so don't overburden your child with too much language.

6 Reach out to choose a fruit or vegetable. Take time to feel it, while at the same time commenting on its shape, size, and texture.

7 Guess the name of the fruit or vegetable and say the name out loud.

8 Remove the eye mask and pass it to your child for her to try. Some children may get upset by the eye mask, in which case simply ask her to close her eyes or cover them with her hands instead.

Other activities to try

Once your child is confident in identifying three different fruits or vegetables, introduce one or two more up to a total of six. Remember to choose ones that have very different textures and shapes, such as a melon, cherry, tomato, pineapple, lemon, grapefruit, kiwi, avocado, carrot, broccoli, or cauliflower.

Introduce vocabulary of size and shape, such as long, short, big, small, thin, fat, round, pointed, crescent.

Slowly introduce more vocabulary comparing the textures. For example, "this is smoother than the orange."

Other describing words you may like to use: soft, softer, softest, hard, rough, bumpy, knobby.

After this activity you could go on to do a sorting activity and sort by fruit and vegetable or shape or color.

I wonder

A child's day is full of wonderment and new experiences, but perhaps the most intriguing of all are new sounds, particularly those that can be heard but whose sources are not at first apparent. This next activity hides an object that produces a sound in a box or container, which when heard, arouses a child's curiosity to find out what is making the sound. This activity works on several levels by refining a child's hearing, extending her knowledge, and developing her finger muscles.

You will need

- Objects for the containers, such as keys, beans, salt or sand, rice, marbles, buttons, Lego pieces, or a teaspoon (you can of course choose your own)
- Containers for the objects: boxes with lids, plastic containers with lids, opaque jars with lids

---

Tip box ■ When you select your first container, choose the one that is the easiest for your child to open.

■ Really emphasize shaking the container close to your ear so she makes the association between hearing and the ears.

SAFETY POINT ⚠ Remember that small objects, such as beads or buttons, can represent a choking hazard for children under three years.

1. Place your objects into the containers you have chosen. Now place the containers on the floor.

2. Sit on the floor next to the containers. Invite your child to come and join you.

3. Look at your child, place your finger on your lips and then to your ear as an indicator that you would like her to be quiet and listen.

4. Explain that you have hidden an object in each of the containers and that she needs to guess what may be in each one.

5. Choose one of the containers, lift it up, and shake it close to your ear.

6. Pass the container to her and let her shake it in the same way to guess which object may be making that sound.

7. If she is having difficulty, tell her the three objects.

8. When she has made her guess, let her open the container to see if her guess was correct.

9. Working in the same way, let her go on to guess the source of the sound in the other containers.

Other activities to try

Once she is confident in guessing three sounds you could add extra containers up to a total of six.

Start with containers that are easy to open, progressing to containers with, for example, screw tops.

When she is confident with guessing the sound and opening all six containers, you could try putting a container within a container.

For the ultimate challenge, you could try giving her a Russian doll and replacing the smallest doll with a small button.

Sort it out

3+ years

Young children love investigating a pile of objects and sorting them into groups. It satisfies their love of order and gives them a lot of information about the world around them.

You will need

- 4–6 different types of large buttons (large enough not to be a choking hazard)
- Enough small containers for each type of button

Tip box ■ Remember that buttons can be a choking hazard, so choose ones as large as possible and supervise your child during this activity.

1 Put a container with all the buttons combined together in the center.

2 Place all the other containers around it in a circle.

3 Ask your child if he thinks all the buttons are the same color and shape.

4 Tell him that he is going to sort them out into the separate containers.

5 Start by putting a button of each type into each container so that it is clear which button needs to go where.

6 Ask your child to sort through the buttons and put them into the correct containers.

7 Once all the buttons have been sorted, he may want to do the activity again.

Other activity to try

Don't just stop at buttons. Plenty of other objects can be used for sorting, such as small pieces of fabric, toy cars, and toy animals.

Coordination

We take very much for granted the ability to move our bodies. The degree of complexity of coordination involved in playing sports and the finer motor skills of using a keyboard or threading a needle in some ways define who we are. Having specialized in teaching Physical Education, I have observed children derive as much pleasure from mastering new physical skills as any language achievement. Control of their bodies gives them a sense of empowerment and self-confidence. In the following chapter you will find activities that will introduce and develop the gross and fine motor skills.

Development timeline: 1½–2 years

In the six months leading to her second birthday, you will see your child's walking begin to improve. By the time she is two, she may even be able to run. Her increased mobility means that she may now manage to climb up, and later also down, a stair with the support of a hand or rail. As she reaches two years old, she may be able to do this without support. She will also be able to start responding to more complex requests such as "give me that toy" and to follow two-step commands.

Your child's speech will have developed so that she will begin to use regularly two or three words together to make sentences and requests of her own, such as "more juice, please."

She will also now have developed a sense of the familiar and will notice if things are out of their regular place, so if, for example, the picture on her bedroom wall is the wrong way around she will

Timeline

able to run

understands
two-step
requests

18 months

imitates the
behavior of
adults

climbs up a
stair holding
onto a hand
or rail

notice. Her sense of balance will be continually improving; she will begin to be able to stand on her tiptoes and by her second birthday should be able to kick a large ball. Her increasing manual dexterity means she can now turn thin paper pages in a book.

With the honing of her observational skills comes the imitation of the behavior of others, in particular adults and older children who are obviously important influences in your child's life.

The following pages will focus on the early stages and development of your child's coordination. Encouraging your child to improve her manual dexterity, balance, and general coordination is important in her early years and will help her achieve her first basic skills. An activity such as Where Does It Go? will not only improve your child's hand-eye coordination and encourage her knowledge of different shapes, it is also a great introduction to simple puzzles. The Circus Performer will help develop your child's sense of balance, while Cardboard Tube Threading will begin to encourage your child's early manual dexterity so that as she grows older she can progress to the more challenging task of Pasta Threading.

21 months

turns thin
paper pages
in a book

uses two or
three words
together

able to stand
on tiptoes

kicks a
large ball

**24
months**

Where does it go?

Hand-eye coordination can be built up from the earliest stages with games that involve the simplest puzzling tasks, starting with fitting squares together and moving toward the more traditional endeavor of making a picture from the separate pieces. This activity shows you how to create materials for the most basic 3D puzzle, which can be developed as your child's skills improve.

You will need

- Collection of different-shaped objects or building blocks, such as a triangle, a square, and a circle
- Cardboard box
- Scissors or craft knife

1 Gather together a number of different-shaped building blocks, such as a triangle, a square, and a circle.

2 Cut holes in the top of the cardboard box that are the same shape as the blocks you have chosen, but make the holes slightly larger. Tape up any open flaps so that there is no other way in except through the holes.

3 Give the first shape to your child. Guide her fingers around the edges, so that she traces the outline of the shape, and then do the same around the hole in the box so that she becomes familiar with the feel of the shape.

4 Ask her to put the shape through the matching hole. If she has trouble finding the correct one, guide her to it.

5 Repeat steps 3 and 4 with the rest of the shapes you have made. When your child is more confident, start again, and see if she can find the correct holes for the shapes on her own.

6 Once your child has become more familiar with the shapes you are using, start to introduce language. When you pass her the shape, say what it is, and relate it back to her knowledge of the way it feels. For example, "This is a triangle. The triangle has three sides."

Other activity to try

Once this has been mastered, you can create variations in the size and shape of the holes and corresponding objects, ideally on the same box, so that the task presents your child with more of a challenge.

Bean bag throwing

2+
years

Bean bags are one of the best pieces of equipment to help young children develop their throwing skills. Unlike a ball, bean bags won't roll away from them, so they feel nice and secure. In this activity the target area for throwing the bean bag is defined to help hand-eye coordination.

1 Lay the rope on the ground and shape it into a circle.

2 Stand about 20 inches (50 cm) away from the rope and demonstrate to your child how to throw the bean bag underarm into the target.

3 Let your child have a try.

4 Once she has mastered this distance, take a step back and let her try it again.

You will need

- Large indoor or outdoor space
- Skipping rope or hoop
- Bean bag or bean-filled soft toy per child

Other activities to try

You could extend the activity by having colored cones and asking her to throw at a particular color.

If there is more than one child, they could see who is first to get their bean bag into the target.

Tip box ■ Remind your child that she needs to keep her arm straight when throwing.

Circus performer

2+ years

We have five senses, but in some ways balance is like a child's sixth sense. Young children seem to have within them an innate longing to develop their balance, and they take any opportunity given to them to walk low beams or along low walls. This activity allows them to pretend to be a circus performer, walking a tightrope, but in complete safety.

1 Find a stone-paved or concrete area where the chalk can be rubbed off.

2 Draw a straight line about 10 feet (3 m) long.

3 Demonstrate to your child how to walk along the line, putting one foot directly in front of the other. Walk with an upright position, eyes forward and arms stretched out horizontally.

4 Let your child have a turn, but he will need your support to guide him in a straight line, so keep hold of both of his outstretched hands as he walks along.

You will need

- Large outdoor space
- Piece of colored chalk

Other activities to try

When he is confident walking the line, he could try holding two flags in each hand. He could also try carrying a small bell, which he has to try not to let ring when walking.

When your child is ready to progress to walking along a low beam or brick wall, let him choose the beam he wants to start with. Children have a very good sense of what height they feel comfortable with.

Building blocks

2+ years

For your child to construct a tower of building blocks in a prescribed order is a real challenge and, when achieved, a major accomplishment. This activity helps to develop this skill and in addition strengthens muscular finger development and hand-eye coordination. It also introduces a child to math with the concept of ordering the blocks according to their shape and size.

1 Ask your child to help you take the building blocks to a clear area on the floor.

2 Sit down with your child on your left, and the blocks slightly to your right.

3 Tell your child that you are going to build the blocks into a tower. Select the largest block and put it in front of you in the center, then slowly complete the rest of the tower, working up to the smallest block at the top.

You will need

- 10 graduated building blocks (Ideally, 2 or 3 of the blocks should be big enough to require your child to carry them with both hands. For a very young child you may want to start with 5 blocks and then work up to 10).

Tip box

■ Be slow and careful in your building of the tower and your child will follow your example.

■ Don't panic if your child cannot achieve the graduated effect the first time. Just building the tower is an accomplishment and in time he will come to recognize that it needs to be graduated.

Other activities to try

The tower is built again but this time the blocks are placed up one corner rather than centrally.

- - - - - - - - - - - - - - - - - - - -

The blocks are used to build a horizontal stair going left to right, smallest to largest.

- - - - - - - - - - - - - - - - - - - -

You could also try this activity using stacking rings with a rod in the middle.

4 Tell your child that you are going to dismantle the tower so that he can build it.

5 Take down the blocks one at a time and place them to the right of your child (he can help you do this). Invite him to build the tower.

Roll a ball

1½+
years

While your toddler may not have yet developed the skills to catch a ball, she will be able to send and receive a ball in a rolling action as introduced in this next activity. It's a great activity for starting to develop those gross motor skills and hand-eye coordination.

1 Sit on the floor with your legs apart so that you are face-to-face with your child.

2 Invite your child to sit in the same way. By sitting in this way you are defining an area and making a barrier for the ball.

3 Begin by gently rolling the ball to your child.

4 Encourage her to stop the ball with her hands. If necessary you may need to demonstrate this.

5 Invite her to roll the ball back to you.

6 When she becomes confident in passing the ball, move yourself back a little farther. This step can be repeated again when she gains confidence at this new distance.

You will need

• Beach ball or similarly large and light ball

Other activity to try

Once she has mastered using the beach ball, you could try changing it for a smaller ball.

Tip box ■ Before you roll the ball to her, briefly look down and then look at her so that she makes the association of looking to the sending point.

Target ball

2+
years

Once your child has mastered sending and receiving a rolling ball, she will now be ready for Target Ball. The degree of coordination is greater, as not only does the ball need to be sent but also, as the name implies, it has to be aimed at a target. The target is filled with water, which adds to the fun factor, but in reality helps to stop the ball from bouncing off target.

1 Place the bowl with the water on the floor. If playing the game indoors, lay down a waterproof sheet first to avoid water damage from splashes.

2 Stand close to the bowl with the ball in your hand and gently throw the ball into the bowl.

3 Pick up the ball and give it to your child. Invite her to try and throw it into the bowl.

4 Once she has been able to reach this target, invite her to step farther back and to try throwing the ball from this new distance. This step can be repeated once she has reached the target from this new distance.

5 Once your child is able to do this from different distances, you can make the activity more challenging by introducing a small- to medium-sized bowl and ball, and repeating steps 1 to 4 with her.

You will need

- Large bowl, something like a washing-up bowl, filled with about 4 inches (10 cm) of water
- Large waterproof sheet (if playing the game indoors)
- Medium to large ball, which needs to be light

Advanced target ball

Now that your child is able to throw a ball at both small and large targets, make the game more challenging by using both sizes in the same game, which will require a degree of visual discrimination.

1 Place the bowls with water on the floor.

2 Put the two balls on the floor near the bowls.

3 Select the large ball.

4 Tell your child that because the big ball has been chosen, it needs to be thrown into the big bowl. Can she find the big bowl?

5 When she has found the big bowl, give her the ball and let her throw it into the bowl.

6 Retrieve the large ball from the bowl.

You will need

- Large light ball
- Small- to medium-sized ball
- Assortment of bowls, large, medium, and small, each filled to about one-third with water
- Waterproof sheet (if playing the game indoors)

Other activities to try

Once your child has mastered this activity, and has understood the concept of big and small, you may like to introduce the term medium-sized by introducing a medium-sized ball and container. To help reinforce this size concept you may like to read to her *Goldilocks and the Three Bears* or *The Three Billy Goats Gruff*.

This activity is an excellent opportunity to introduce the language of opposites: big, small, large, little, biggest, smallest, bigger, smaller. Remember, though, that the language is merely helping to give a clearer understanding of the activity so don't let your child feel swamped by it.

7 Now select the smaller ball.

8 Tell your child that because the small ball has been chosen, it needs to be thrown into the small bowl. Can she find the small bowl?

9 When she has found the smaller bowl, give her the ball and let her throw it into the bowl.

10 Continue the activity until all the target bowls have been tried.

11 Once she can confidently manage to achieve all of the targets, invite her to step back a little farther away from the bowls. This step can be repeated once she has achieved the targets from this new distance.

Tip box

■ Remember that all children take their own time to master a new skill, and it may be that your child will not be able to achieve all the targets the first time.

■ When your child is choosing which ball to use, give her time and don't be tempted to jump in and tell her the answer.

Cardboard tube threading

1½+ years

Here's another excellent simple activity that your child will find endlessly absorbing and will provide another opportunity for developing hand-eye coordination and strengthening finger muscles. It also has the added advantage of being very easy to prepare.

1 Start by tying the bell or small object to one end of the chain. This will act as a stop for the tube and prevent it from coming off the chain.

2 Put the chain on the floor or a low table.

3 Cut the tube in half.

4 Demonstrate to your child how to thread the tube onto the chain and slide it back and forth.

5 Remove the tube from the chain and allow your child to have a try.

You will need

- Small bell or tennis ball or any small object wider than the end of the tube
- Chain or cord about 3 feet (1 m) in length (you could even use the belt from a robe)
- Knife to cut the tube
- Cardboard tube (the type you have on the inside of a kitchen paper towel roll)

Tip box ■ When demonstrating this activity, your child needs to sit to the left of you so that she can have an unrestricted view of your hands. If your child is left-handed you will need to demonstrate with your left hand, and your child will also need to sit on the right side of you.

Pasta threading

When your child has mastered Cardboard Tube Threading, she is now ready to move on to pasta threading, which requires a greater degree of fine motor skills.

You will need

- Several pieces of string, approximately 20 inches (50 cm) in length
- Packet of rigatoni pasta (tube shapes)

1 Put out the pieces of string and pasta either on a low table or on the floor.

2 Invite your child to join you and explain that you are going to show her how to thread the pasta tubes onto the string.

3 Take a piece of pasta and thread it onto the string. When you get a few inches from the end, knot the string around the pasta so that the first piece of pasta acts as a stop for the rest of the chain.

4 Demonstrate to your child how to thread a piece of pasta onto the string.

5 Now give her a piece of pasta to thread.

6 Let her continue threading the pasta until the string is full.

Tip box ■ When you first try this activity with your child, make sure to choose the largest tube-shaped pasta that is available.

You could make your string of pasta into jewelry—all you need is some food coloring.

1 Add a teaspoon of food coloring to a bowl or deep baking tray filled with water.

2 Holding both ends of the pasta string, pass it to your child and explain that she needs to dip it into the colored water so that the pasta is covered.

3 Remind her that she needs to keep hold of the string.

4 Keep the pasta in the water for a couple of minutes so that it is stained with the color.

5 Ask her to remove the pasta from the water.

6 Take the pasta string and hang it up to dry, putting a sheet of paper underneath to catch any drips.

Other activity to try

You could do two strings of pasta, each of a different color. When both strings have dried, they can be rethreaded onto a new string to make a necklace of two different colors.

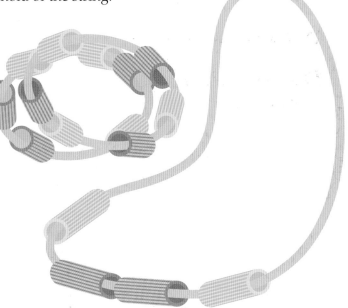

Arts and crafts

Love of creating seems to be an innate desire that is within all of us from the very earliest of ages. If young children are encouraged in their creative endeavors, it provides an important source of self-confidence and satisfaction. It matters not that you may only see blobs of color on a page because for them it is their way of making their mark and saying who they are. In the following chapter, you will find a variety of art and craft activities that will satisfy every young budding artist.

Development timeline: 2–2½ years

Unlike his first birthday, your child will be actively aware of his second birthday and it will be consciously marked by him as well as you, his parents. During the next six months, he will continue to develop his early basic skills. So, for example, he will be beginning to sort objects he is given into categories of shape and color. Your child may start potty training at any time between eighteen months and three years old. The exact time will really depend on the child. Boys do tend to start later, but if he is aware that others of his age have already started then this can be a positive impetus.

From the age of two upward, your child may also be learning how to ride a small tricycle, although this skill can be very variable as some children will find the alternating motion more difficult to master.

At this age your child will begin to enjoy being around and playing with other children, although cooperative play and taking turns will come later, so there may still be fights over particular favored toys.

Timeline

begins to sort
objects by shape
and color

potty
training

24 months

enjoys playing
with other
children

beginnings of
make-believe
play

At this point you may also notice the beginnings of make-believe play as he begins to use his imagination.

Routine is very important to children at this age. Although he will not really understand the concept of times and routines, he is likely to notice and protest at any big changes to his daily schedule. So, for example, if you go on vacation it is vital that you ensure bedtime and mealtimes remain as normal as possible, otherwise excitement at being somewhere new may well boil over into tantrums.

Art and craft activities can be extremely important in encouraging your child's development, not just for his creative output but also for increasing his knowledge of colors, his manual skills with holding crayons and scissors, and a whole range of other skills he can learn as he creates. Your child will be able to develop his coordination through telling stories with fingers while also learning numbers with the Counting Gloves. As well as having fun at the Pizza Parlor, he will be strengthening his finger muscles with the dough and exercising his imagination. While he is creating toys to float at bath time with Floating Fun, he will also be learning about objects that sink and float.

starts to ride
a tricycle

able to
throw a ball
overhand

27 months

objects to
big changes
in routine

**30
months**

Painting with water

1½+
years

When children paint they are confined to a sheet of paper, but painting outside with water means every surface can be their canvas. They don't worry that there is no paint involved; as far as they are concerned, they are making their mark. Parents love this activity too as it involves no clearing up!

1 Explain to your child that he is going to paint, but instead of painting onto paper he can paint onto any surface that he likes, such as a tree trunk.

2 Hand your child a paintbrush and watch him go.

You will need

- Paintbrush (such as a small brush for painting woodwork) per child
- Container for the water, preferably with a handle

Tip box ■ You may have certain no-go areas in your outdoor space, in which case give very clear instructions about where he is allowed to go.

Floor art

2+
years

This brilliant activity gives children a large space to be creative, so they are not restricted to a regular size or shape of paper. And who says only hands can draw—feet dipped in paint might be just as good, and will again encourage different approaches to creativity.

1 Tape the paper to a clean area of floor (preferably linoleum or something wipe-clean) that is free from hazards and valuable furniture.

2 Use as much space as you can, the point of this project is to have an adventure exploring and marking the surface of the paper, without the usual limits.

3 Line up the art materials and let your child choose one. Direct her to the paper, as she may be a little hesitant at first.

4 Don't be afraid to join in and create patterns and stories together.

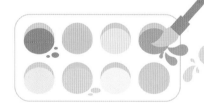

You will need

- Masking tape
- Poster paper
- Crayons, felt-tip pens, paint

Tip box   ■ Fill an empty, washed out roll-on deodorant stick with thinned poster paint to create giant pens that can be grasped in two hands.

Potato prints

2+ years

Gloriously messy and fun, this is an opportunity for your child to explore colors and textures while creating beautiful patterns.

1 Wash the potatoes and dry them.

2 Prepare your area for painting by laying down newspaper and squeezing the paint into shallow trays. Wear old clothes or an apron.

3 Cut the potatoes in half and show your child how to dip them in the paint and press them gently on the paper.

4 Let her experiment with the colors and with the different patterns provided by the potatoes.

5 Invite your child to pin them to the wall once dry.

You will need

- Baking potatoes
- Newspaper
- Water-based paint in different colors
- Shallow trays
- Knife
- Large sheets of paper

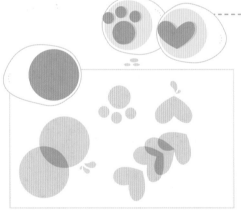

Tip box ■ Once your child has done this activity with the natural shape of the potato, try carving into it with a knife to create more interesting shapes.

Spray paint

2+ years

Children are fascinated with using a pump spray as a means of applying paint. They adore watching the spray of paint coming out. They also enjoy having such a large surface area of paper to work on.

1 Mix up the paints to a very runny consistency.

2 Pour the paints into the pump-spray bottles.

3 Take the sprays outside, along with the roll of wallpaper-lining paper, scissors, and stones.

4 Cut a long length of paper and weigh down the edges with stones.

5 Ask your child to put on an apron and show her how to use the pump spray.

6 Stand back and let her spray away.

You will need

- Outdoor area
- 4 different colors of water-based or poster paint
- 4 plastic pump-spray bottles
- Roll wallpaper-lining paper or butcher's paper
- Scissors
- Some stones to act as paperweights
- Apron per child

Tip box ■ The finished painting could act as a backdrop for a further art project, such as a seascape.

Hands on

Children love the sensation of covering their hands with paint and this activity lets them do exactly that. They make handprints using paint and then turn them into a piece of art.

You will need

- Plastic tablecloth or newspaper
- Poster or powder paint mixed thickly in 2 or 3 bright colors of your choice
- Pots to mix up powder paint
- Apron for each child
- 2 sheets of 11- by 17-inch paper per paint color
- Plastic tray or shallow dish for each color
- Spoons for mixing
- Area to spread the paper when drying
- Scissors

1 Cover your work surface with the cloth or newspaper.

2 If using powder paint, mix with water to make a paint with the consistency of household paint.

3 Explain to your child that he is going to be doing some handprints.

4 Ask him to put on his apron.

5 Put the paper and the trays on the table.

6 Start with one color and let him help pour it into a tray. Spread it out using the back of a spoon.

7 Ask him to spread out his hand and put it into the paint, and then transfer it to the paper.

8 Repeat the process until two sheets of paper are covered with handprints.

9 Ask him to wash his hands and start all over again with a new color.

10 When all the sheets are covered with handprints, allow to dry.

Tip box ■ Do not use blue paint for the handprints if you will be using your child's handprints for the angelfish activity on page 58, as the background for that will be blue.

Angelfish handprints

3+ years

Using a collection of your child's handprints, you can turn them into a new piece of art, like these angelfish made from cutouts of the handprints.

1 Place the butcher's paper on a table and weigh it down at the corners.

2 Mix up the blue powder paint or water down the poster paint to a wash consistency.

3 Using the sponge, show your child how to dip it in the paint and then spread it onto the paper with a sweeping wave action.

4 When all the paper is covered with the blue wash, allow to dry.

5 Take one of the cutout handprints and ask your child to put glue on the non-painted side of the palm.

You will need

- Wallpaper-lining paper or butcher's paper, about 31–40 inches (80–100 cm)
- Blue poster or powder paint
- Household sponge cut into about a 4-inch (10-cm) square
- Area to spread the paper when drying
- Cutout handprints (see pages 56–57)
- Glue stick
- Colored felt-tip pens

Tip box ■ Remember to let your child go at his own pace. It might take several stages to complete.

6 Let him stick it anywhere on the blue painted paper.

7 Take another hand in another color and stick it on top of the first hand with a slight overlap, ensuring that you have the fingers all going in the same way.

8 If you have a third color, repeat with that.

9 The fingers on the handprint should give the impression of a feathery fan.

10 Let your child make several fish to fill the blue area.

11 Show him how he can make eyes on the fish using the felt-tip pens.

12 When it is finished, pin it up so that he can admire his handiwork.

Other activities to try

Of course, the possibilities are endless for decorating the fish. You might like to use shells, seaweed, and/or glitter paint.

You might like to read together the story *The Rainbow Fish* by Marcus Pfister before or after this activity.

Finger fun

2+ years

We take our hands and the skills we employ them for very much for granted; for a child, hands are a key tool in her development. This next activity is a fun art project that, when completed, can be used in both language and counting activities. It requires little more than a pair of old gloves and some Velcro. I'm going to give you the instructions for creating Story Gloves and Counting Gloves.

You will need

- Pair of scissors
- Crayons or felt-tip pens
- Glue stick
- Some pieces of cardboard (not too thick)
- Strip of peel-off Velcro about 12 inches (30 cm) long
- Pair of woolly gloves

Tip box

■ Remember to have the bears and Goldilocks on separate hands.
■ Remember to use gloves that will fit your child's hands.

■ If you are going to use the gloves for another story, there is no need to peel off the Velcro already on the gloves.

Story Gloves

1 At the back of the book on page 154 you will find the characters for the story *Goldilocks and the Three Bears*. Photocopy this page and cut out the figures.

2 Ask your child to color in the figures.

3 Ask her to glue the figures onto the cardboard and allow the glue to dry.

4 Cut out the figures.

5 Cut the Velcro into 1-inch (2-cm) pieces.

6 Stick the Velcro on one side at the back of the figure, and the other corresponding piece on a finger of one of the gloves.

7 Repeat until all the figures have been backed with Velcro, with corresponding pieces on the gloves.

8 The gloves are now ready to be used for a storytelling session of *Goldilocks and the Three Bears*.

Other activity to try

The Story Gloves can be used for many other stories; here are just a few suggestions: *The Three Billy Goats Gruff; The Three Little Pigs; Little Red Riding Hood.*

Counting Gloves

1. On page 155 you will find templates for cupcakes. Photocopy these and cut them out.

2. Draw around the cupcake templates onto scraps of fabric. Make ten cupcakes.

3. Cut out the cupcakes and ask your child to glue them onto the cardboard. Allow the glue to dry.

4. Cut out the cardboard cupcakes.

5. Ask your child to mark the top of each cupcake with a red spot to represent a cherry using a red felt-tip pen.

6. Stick one piece of Velcro on the back of a cupcake and the corresponding piece on the finger of the glove.

7. Repeat until all the cupcakes have been backed and all the corresponding pieces of Velcro stuck on the gloves.

8. The gloves are now ready for the counting song. Start by using just one glove.

You will need

- The same items used for the Story Gloves
- Some scraps of fabric—I like to use felt, as it does not fray
- Red felt-tip pen
- Glue strong enough to stick fabric

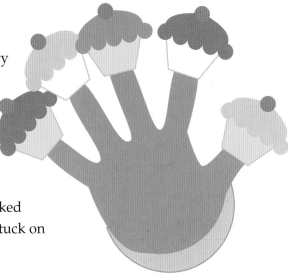

Five Fairy Cakes in a Baker's Shop

Five fairy cakes in a baker's shop
Round and fat with a cherry on the top.
Along came (insert name) *with a penny one day,*
She/he bought a fairy cake and took it right away.

> Invite your child to remove one of the cakes and count how many are left.
> Repeat the song again but this time begin with four fairy cakes.
> Invite your child to remove one of the cakes and count how many are left.
> Repeat until you get down to one.

One fairy cake in a baker's shop,
One fairy cake with a cherry on the top.
Along came (insert name) *with a penny one day,*
She/he bought a fairy cake and there are zero left today.

Other activities to try

When your child is confident in counting down from five, begin at six, then seven and right up to ten.

The Counting Gloves can be used for plenty of other counting songs—here are just a few: *Five Green and Speckled Frogs; Five Green Bottles Hanging on a Wall;* and *Five Little Monkeys Jumping on the Bed.* You'll need to create your own cutout figures for these.

Tip box

■ When counting the remaining cakes, take time with the counting so that your child understands that it is one count per cake.

■ When the cake is removed, it may be easier for your child to physically put down her finger so that she can quite clearly see that the cake is gone.

Homemade play dough

2+ years

There is no better way to strengthen finger muscles than by playing with dough—and play dough can be used for a whole range of fun games and activities.

You will need

- 1 cup of plain flour
- 1/2 cup of salt
- 2 teaspoons of cream of tartar
- 1 cup of water
- 1 teaspoon of food coloring
- 2 teaspoons of cooking oil
- Medium saucepan
- Wooden spoon

1. Put the flour, salt, and cream of tartar into a medium saucepan and stir together with a wooden spoon.

2. Over a medium heat, gradually stir in the water, food coloring, and oil.

3. Keep stirring continually as the mixture begins to cook and forms into a sticky ball.

4. Remove from heat.

5. Cool for 15–30 minutes.

6. The recipe will make enough dough for two children to create a Pizza Parlor (see opposite).

Tip box ■ The dough can be stored for several days in a plastic bag in the fridge.

Pizza parlor

3+ years

All young children love pizza and playing with dough. This activity combines the two. By creating their own pizza parlor they have a framework in which to exercise their imaginative and role-playing ideas. This is best done with several children.

You will need

- Play dough (see opposite for recipe)
- Sheet of paper per child, plus 4 extra sheets
- Colored felt-tip pens
- Old pizza boxes
- Glue stick
- 2 protective cloths for work and parlor areas
- Apron per child
- If possible, a child-sized rolling pin for each child (if you don't have any rolling pins, use something like a plastic cup)
- Plastic knives
- Paper plates

1 Start by making the dough. (You may want to make more than one batch of play dough, using different colors for the pizza dough and the toppings.)

2 Explain to the children that they are going to make their own pizza parlor.

3 Write out a sign and labels for the parlor. Stick the labels onto the boxes and put the sign in the work area.

4 Write out a menu offering four varieties of pizza on a piece of paper. Tell the children what the choices are.

5 Put a protective tablecloth on the work area. Ask the children to put on their aprons and help you set out the dough and the tools.

6 On another table put out the other protective tablecloth and ask the children to help set out the paper plates for the customers.

7 If there are several children, divide them into two groups—the pizza makers and the customers. (They can swap over after awhile.) Otherwise, prevail upon any available adults to be customers.

PIZZA MENU

MARGARITA
HAWAIIAN
PEPPERONI
FOUR CHEESE

Tip box

■ After the activity, check the bottom of your children's shoes. Dough sticks very easily to the soles.

■ Remind your children that this dough is definitely not for eating.

8 Ask the pizza makers to first take orders from the customers. Help them to make a mark on the pizza menu next to the pizza selected.

9 Ask the children to make their pizza and, when finished, put it into the box and give it to the customer.

10 When everyone has had an opportunity to make some pizza, close the pizza parlor and ask everyone to help clean up. The dough can be stored back in the bags and kept in the fridge to use again.

Other activity to try

Once your child has played this, you may like to vary the game by changing the setting. Instead of a pizza parlor, it could be a tea shop, and your child could make little cupcakes for all of her customers.

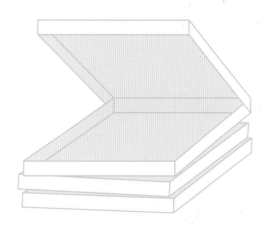

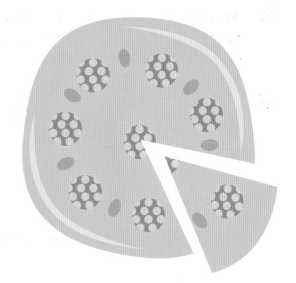

Make a scarecrow

3+ years

Children love making this fun scarecrow model and will engage in the process of building up a character from scratch. There is plenty of opportunity for exploring concepts of color and texture with your child, as well as learning words for clothing and parts of the body. The action of stuffing will also encourage your child's dexterity. This is a great activity at Halloween, and it makes a fun outside excursion to put your scarecrow in the garden.

1 Gather all your chosen materials together on the floor or at a low table.

2 Invite your child to join you. Tell him you're going to make a scarecrow together.

3 First you need to stuff the pair of tights. Straw is a great material to stuff the tights with, and makes your scarecrow more authentic, but you could use almost anything. Show your child how to scrunch up your chosen material and stuff it right down into the feet of the tights.

You will need

- Pair of children's tights
- Material for stuffing (this can be straw, newspaper, socks, cotton, wool, or any other materials you have at hand)
- String
- Old shirt or sweater
- Marker
- Other clothing for your scarecrow (optional)

Tip box ■ A pair of children's tights is best for this activity as it keeps the scarecrow at a more manageable size for your child, but you can also use a pair of adult tights.

4 Let your child have a try. You may need to help him push the stuffing all the way down.

5 When the tights are completely stuffed, you need to tie a piece of string around the very top of the tights, at the waistband, to seal it off and stop the stuffing from falling out.

6 To create a head for the scarecrow, tie another piece of string around him, halfway between the waistband and the top of the legs, and secure it tightly so that you separate a head from the body.

7 Dress the scarecrow with the shirt or sweater (this will need to be small—either an old one belonging to your child, or even one temporarily borrowed from a doll or teddy bear).

8 Stuff the arms of the sweater with more of your stuffing material, and then tie them off at the ends to create arms for the scarecrow.

9 Now tell your child that he needs to give the scarecrow a face. Talk to your child about what sort of face he would like to give the scarecrow—will he have a smile or a scary frown?

10 Then, if he is able, give your child the marker to draw eyes and a mouth on your scarecrow's face.

11 If you prefer not to draw on the tights, you could cut out paper shapes and glue them on for the face instead. Cut out shapes for the eyes and mouth, and let your child color them in before gluing them on.

12 If you have any other old clothes, put these on the scarecrow. A brimmed hat is an especially effective accessory. If you have been using straw as your stuffing material, you could also stick any leftover straw on your scarecrow for a more authentic look.

13 Your scarecrow is now complete and ready to participate in a scarecrow song or story. Turn to page 95 for the "Dingle-Dangle Scarecrow" song.

Other activity to try

If you have a wooden pole, you could attach it to the back of your scarecrow, through the back of the shirt, to make him stand upright. You will need to do this if you want to take your scarecrow outside and place him in the garden.

Floating fun

2+ years

Children like having toys to play with in the bath, and this activity adds to the fun, letting them create their own toys while at the same time learning about objects that sink and float.

1 Gather your materials on the floor or a low table. Invite your child to sit with you.

2 Ask her "What floats in water?" She might reply "boats," or with the names of marine animals.

3 Draw her ideas on the Styrofoam and cut them out with the craft knife, being careful to keep your child's hands out of the way.

4 Use the skewer to make a hole in each object and let your child thread them together to form a flotilla.

5 At bath time, set the flotilla off and let your child play with the creation, trying to sink it with waves and marveling as it floats to the surface.

SAFETY POINT !
Never leave your child unaccompanied around water, even for a very short period of time.

You will need

- Pieces of Styrofoam
- Pen
- Craft knife
- Skewer
- String
- Full bathtub

Other activity to try

Emphasize the contrast between floating and sinking objects by bringing some heavy ones along to bath time. Drop them in the water and explore their journey with your child.

This activity doesn't have to be restricted to bath time. If you have a pond in your garden or nearby, you can take your flotilla on an adventure there too.

Flying fish

3+
years

This game combines two activities in one. First the child makes and designs his fish, then he learns how to propel it with the aid of a newspaper. If there is more than one child, or if you make one as well, you can race the fish.

You will need

- Photocopy of the fish template from page 156, one for each child
- Colored pencils, crayons, or felt-tip pens
- Scissors
- Rolled-up newspaper or magazine for each child

Tip box ■ Remember to use a non-carpeted floor. Wood or laminate is best.

1 Explain that you are going to make some flying fish.

2 Give each child a photocopy of the fish and ask them to color it in.

3 Help them cut out the fish.

4 Put a finished fish onto a non-carpeted floor.

5 Using a rolled-up newspaper or magazine, demonstrate how to propel the fish along by beating the air behind it.

6 Let each child have a try.

7 Once they have managed to propel their fish, organize all the fish along a starting line to have a fish race.

Treasure map

For children of any age there seems to be a universal appeal in following a trail that leads to treasure. Forget expensive electronic toys and make a treasure map instead. It will give far more pleasure, it won't break down, and your children will never tire of playing a game that involves treasure.

1 Start by making some tea in a pot and let it cool.

2 While it is cooling, look at some maps with your child. Talk about how maps are used to find your way. Explain that the blue on a map represents water.

3 You can use the template on page 157 as a starting point for your map and add your own features, or you can simply start with a blank piece of paper and do it all from scratch. If using the template, photocopy it onto 11- by 17-inch paper.

4 Tell him that he is going to make his own old map that will help find treasure.

You will need

- 2 tea bags
- Teapot
- Examples of maps from an atlas or other books
- Template of treasure map on page 157 (optional)
- Sheet of 11- by 17-inch paper (if there is more than one child allow one sheet per child)
- Large bowl
- Colored felt-tip pens or crayons

Tip box ■ Remember that it is going to take a while to complete the map, allowing for soaking and drying time. This is an activity to do throughout the day.

5 When the tea is cool, pour it into the bowl. Show him how to tear the edges of the paper and then fold it up and put into the bowl. Ask him what color he thinks the paper will be when it is left in the tea. Let the paper soak for about two hours.

6 Help him to lift out the paper gently, removing any excess water and spreading it out to dry.

7 When dry, explain to him that the treasure is going to be hidden on an island.

8 Help him to draw an outline for the island and ask him what he is going to call it. Write the name of the island on the map.

9 Ask him where the treasure is to be hidden and to make a cross at that point. Explain to him that he needs to make a dotted trail to the cross.

10 Fill in the map with things like a treasure chest, palm trees, a shipwreck, shark fins, an alligator swamp, quicksand, mermaids, dolphins, and whales. Color the water areas in blue.

Other activity to try

Your map is now ready for an adventure! See The Pirate Game on page 106.

Games and movement

Is there any greater joy for a child than the joy of moving to music or the thrill of an imaginary game played with others? These simple pleasures can go a long way toward helping your child's development in coordination, listening skills, following and remembering instructions, and the ability to cooperate with others. In the following chapter, you will find everything from dancing with balloons to making your own bowling alley.

Development timeline: 2½–3 years

In the months leading up to her third birthday, your child is becoming increasingly mobile, which means that she may now be able to walk up and down stairs holding on to the banister. Her dexterity will have improved to the extent that she is able to use a pair of children's scissors to cut paper, and she may even be able to help with dressing. By the time she is three years old, her command of balance will have improved to the point where she can stand on one foot.

By now your child's sense of adventure will have been boosted by the ability to open doors, so she could be anywhere! This means that you will need to keep a close eye on her, and keep any doors you don't want her to go through firmly locked, so that her adventures don't lead her outside the house without your knowledge. The honing of her motor skills means that she will now be able to stack objects in size order. Potty training should now be in full swing, and she will certainly be

Timeline

walks up and down stairs without support

uses sentences of five to six words

30 months

able to name some colors

33 months

advanced enough to tell others when she needs the toilet.

Your child's language skills will also be improving. She will generally be asking and responding to a variety of simple questions and she will be starting to use longer sentences of five or six words. She will mostly be understood by family members when she speaks, although strangers may have more difficulty discerning her words. She will be starting to name some colors, and may even be starting to count, at least able to repeat the words, even if she does not yet fully understand the concept of numbers properly at this point.

The activities in this chapter are ideal for your child at this age. Not only will she enjoy the fun of the energetic games, but activities such as Dancing to Music and the Traffic Lights Game will also help to develop her increasing mobility and movement. As most of these activities are best played with a group of children of three or more—especially the games such as The Island Game and The Pirate Game—they will also encourage her interaction with other children, while Role Play will promote cooperative play and also help her to exercise her growing imagination.

able to use
a pair of
children's
scissors

1 2 3

36 months

can mostly be
understood by
family members
when speaking

beginning
to count

able to stand
on one foot

Dancing to music

2+
years

Children love nothing better than dancing to music. They enjoy being able to express themselves through the music, and their pleasure is extended if there is more than one child. For parents nothing could be simpler than just providing the music, with the knowledge that your child is having so much fun and pleasure, and at the same time getting some exercise.

Dancing with scarves

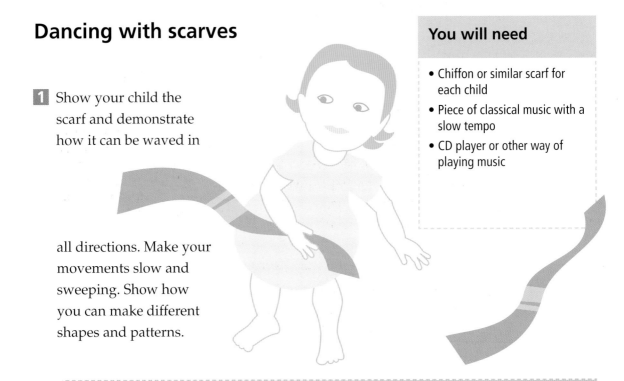

1 Show your child the scarf and demonstrate how it can be waved in

You will need

- Chiffon or similar scarf for each child
- Piece of classical music with a slow tempo
- CD player or other way of playing music

all directions. Make your movements slow and sweeping. Show how you can make different shapes and patterns.

Tip box ■ You could also try this activity with ribbons.

2 Let your child have a try with the scarf.

3 Put on the music and move together to the music. Encourage your child to move lightly on her toes, while remembering to keep waving her scarf.

Dancing to different tempos

1 Put on the music and encourage your child to listen to the different tempos.

2 Together move to the music.

3 Encourage her to think not only about moving in time to the different speeds, but also how the movement changes. Lighter movements for the faster sections, heavier movements for the slower sections.

4 When she is confident with changing the speed of her movement to match the music, encourage her to think about the different directions: backward, forward, turning, and zigzag, all of which should be demonstrated first.

Other activities to try

Once she has mastered the movement with one scarf, give your child a second scarf.

- -

Once she is confident in her movements, encourage her to work at different levels: up high and down low.

You will need

- Piece of music that changes tempo, such as *The Carnival of Animals* by Camille Saint-Saëns, or *Morning In the Hall of the Mountain King* by Edvard Grieg from the play *Peer Gynt*

Dances with stories

1 Begin by telling or reading the story.

2 Listen to the music.

3 Work through the different stages of the story with your child, devising clear, simple movements that match the story.

4 You may need to recap certain stages of the story.

You will need

- Music with stories, such as *The Ugly Duckling* by Hans Christian Andersen (music by Frank Loesser), *The Three Little Fish* by Saxie Dowell, or *Peter and the Wolf* by Sergei Prokofiev
- CD player or other way of playing music

Other activity to try

You could also find some appropriate music to go with your child's favorite story. Many children love dancing the story of *The Very Hungry Caterpillar* by Eric Carle.

Tip box ■ Let your child contribute as much as possible when deciding on the movements for the story.

Dancing to a theme

1 Let your child listen to the music first. See if she can work out the different types of weather that might be expressed throughout the piece of music.

- Music with a theme, such as Beethoven's *Pastoral Symphony* (weather), or a piece of music with a strong, slow beat, such as *The Skater's Waltz* by Emile Waldteufel
- CD player or other way of playing music

2 Show how a dance can tell a story to match the music. Start with a nice day, then you need to put up your imaginary umbrella as the rain falls. You might jump over puddles and finally run to avoid a storm.

3 Let her try the action.

4 Move together around the room to the music.

5 Vary the music to introduce different themes, such as skating to music. Again let your child listen to the music first to get the "feel" of it.

6 Demonstrate a skating action with swinging pendulum arms and long sliding steps.

7 Let your child try the action, and then move around the room together.

8 Once she is confident with the movement, introduce different directions and turns.

Dancing with balloons

1 Show your child the balloon and demonstrate to her how to bat the balloon with the palm of the hand to keep it up in the air. The idea is to keep the balloon up in the air as long as possible, while dancing to the music. This should help your child to develop a sense of rhythm and encourage light movements.

2 Let her try.

3 Put on the music and encourage her to keep her eye on the balloon as she bats it up.

4 As she gets more confident, encourage her to bat the balloon a bit higher and to move around the room.

You will need

- Balloon for each child
- Piece of classical music with a slow tempo
- CD player or other way of playing music

Tip box   ■ A burst balloon can be very disappointing for a child, so have some spare balloons ready.

The animal game

Children are fascinated by animals and the different movements and sounds they make, and this game allows them to explore these. It is simple to play, and it doesn't require any props. This is an excellent activity as a follow-up from a trip to a zoo or a farm.

1 Tell your child he is going to play The Animal Game, and he has to act like the animal you show him.

2 Animal picture cards or toy models are a fun accessory to this game, but they are not necessary to play. If you are using them, pick one up and show it to your child. If not, you can just tell him the name of an animal. Make sure you only choose animals that he will be familiar with, especially for younger children.

3 Ask your child to show you what noise that animal makes. If he has any trouble with this at first, make the noise yourself and ask him to copy you.

4 Ask him to pretend he is that animal and move around the room. Again, if he has trouble doing this, you can get him started. For example, as an elephant you might use one of your arms to swing like a trunk, or for a penguin, put your feet together and waddle forward.

You will need

- Picture cards of a variety of animals, or a selection of animal toy models (optional)

Other activity to try

You could also play a "who am I?" version of this game. Make the movements and the sounds of an animal and ask your child to guess what animal you are.

The island game

2+ years

Children love games that involve finding a safe place or base. In this game the safe place is represented by a newspaper island, which they must get to when the word "shark" is called out. This game also has the advantage that it requires minimal resources and preparation. It works best when you have a group of at least three children.

You will need

- Large indoor or outdoor space
- Old newspaper
- Scissors

1 If the newspaper is large (as in a broadsheet), cut each double sheet into two. If it is small (as in a tabloid), then there is no need to cut it.

2 Set out the pieces of paper over the area where the game is to be played, ensuring that there is enough space around each piece of paper so that the children can run around it safely without bumping into one another or any obstacles in the room.

3 Explain to the children that the pieces of paper represent islands around which they must "swim" until they hear the word "shark," when they must jump onto an island.

4 Remind the children that they must go around the islands, not across them and to be aware of other children as they move around.

Other activity to try

You also could play a musical version of this game. The children should "swim" around the islands while the music is playing. When it stops they must jump onto an island.

Tip box
■ You could use hoops instead of newspaper to make the islands.

■ Older children would also enjoy joining in this game.

Fruit salad

2+ years

This is a very simple fun game that children really respond to. It's a great way for them to burn off excess energy, and it has the added advantage of requiring no resources. You need a group of three or more children to play this.

1 Ask the children to come into the center of your designated space and tell them that they are going to play the game of Fruit Salad.

2 Point to each of the four corners of the space and give each corner the name of a fruit. For example, "This is the strawberry corner," "This is the apple corner," and so on.

3 Explain to the children that when you call out the name of a fruit, they all have to run to that corner.

4 Also tell them that when you call out "Fruit salad," they need to run to the center.

You will need

• Large indoor or outdoor space

Tip box ■ You might want to use colored cones or markers to mark each corner as a different fruit, so that the children don't forget which corner represents which fruit.

5 Repeat again which corner is which fruit and then just point to each corner and ask the children to tell you the name, so you can make sure they all know which corner is which.

6 Start the game by calling out the first fruit of your choice. Give the children time to get to the corner before calling out the next fruit and repeating until everyone is tired of the game!

You don't have to stick with names of fruits. You could use colors and call the center of the space the "rainbow."

If the children are getting breathless from running, or you want to vary the game, you could call out different actions, such as, "Walk backward to the banana corner."

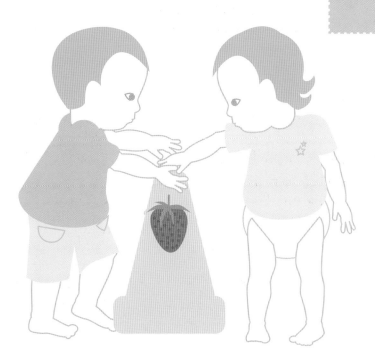

Bowling alley

2+
years

Your children can have their own bowling alley in their home with this very easy-to-prepare bowling game. They will enjoy seeing the pins tumble as they hit them with a rolling ball. This game can be played individually, in pairs, or in teams. It's also a great game for improving hand-eye coordination.

You will need

- Long narrow indoor or outdoor space, about 13 by 3 feet (4 by 1 m)
- 5 large empty water or soft-drink bottles with lids
- Lightweight medium-sized ball

Tip box ■ You could decorate the pins with colored stickers or number the pins with a marker.

■ If the pins seem a little unstable, you could fill them with a little water or with rice to weigh them down.

1 Set all of the pins up in a row at one end of your chosen space.

2 Ask the children to stand at the other end.

3 You could line cushions down the sides of the alley to clearly define the path for the children.

4 Demonstrate to them how to roll the ball to try to knock down the pins.

5 Let them take turns trying to knock down the pins and helping to set them up again for the next player.

Other activity to try

Once the children become more confident with this game and are able to knock down more of the pins, you could change the formation to make it more challenging for them.

The kitchen band

Open up your kitchen cupboards and you will find that your pots, pans, and wooden spoons can serve as excellent makeshift instruments. Your children will delight to hear the sounds they produce when they hit each surface. This activity works well with one child or with many.

You will need

- Selection of pots and pans including at least 2 lids
- Wooden spoons
- Soft cloth
- Metal spoons
- Sheet of wax paper
- Jar of dried beans

1 Set out the objects to be used as musical instruments. Show the children how the "instruments" can be used.

2 The wooden spoon can be used to hit the top of the saucepans, like a drum.

3 The two lids can act as cymbals.

4 The soft cloth can be wrapped around one of the wooden spoons. This wrapped spoon will produce a softer sound when striking a saucepan lid.

5 The cupped parts of the two metal spoons can be hit together to make a noise.

6 The wax paper can be folded and used to make a noise by pressing your lips against it and blowing.

7 The jar of dried beans can be held and shaken.

8 Once they have mastered the "instruments," you can introduce the children to the song. See page 94 for "I Am the Music Man."

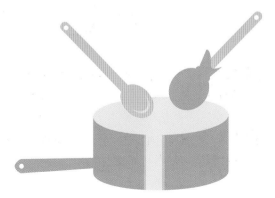

The Music Man

Now that your instruments and your Kitchen Band are assembled (see page 92), the children are ready for the music. While playing their "instruments," they can join in with the song "I Am the Music Man."

I am the Music Man
I come from down your
  way
And I can play
I play piano

Pi-a, pi-a, pi-an-o
Pi-an-o, pi-an-o
Pi-a, pi-a, pi-an-o
Pi-a, pi-an-o.

Pi-an-o, pi-an-o
Pi-a, pi-a, pi-an-o
Pi-a, pi-an-o.

Repeat the first verse but with the last line:
. . . the saxophone.

Sax-o, sax-o, sax-o-phone
Sax-o-phone, sax-o-phone
Sax-o, sax-o, sax-o-phone
Sax-o, sax-o-phone.

Sax-o-phone, sax-o-phone
Sax-o, sax-o, sax-o-phone
Sax-o, sax-o-phone.

Pi-an-o, pi-an-o
Pi-a, pi-a, pi-an-o
Pi-a, pi-an-o.

Repeat the first verse but with the last line:
. . . the big bass drum.

Big bass, big bass, big bass
  drum
Big bass drum, big bass
  drum
Big bass, big bass, big bass
  drum
Big bass, big bass drum.

Big bass drum, big bass
  drum
Big bass, big bass, big bass
  drum
Big bass, big bass drum.

Repeat the three-line saxophone chorus and then the three-line piano chorus.

Repeat the music man verse but the last line is:
. . . I play the triangle.

Tri-a, tri-a, triangle
Triangle, triangle
Tri-a, tri-a, triangle
Tri-a, triangle.

Triangle, triangle
Tri-a, tri-a, triangle
Tri-a, triangle.

Repeat the three-line big bass drum chorus followed by the saxophone three-line chorus.

Pi-an-o, pi-an-o
Pi-a, pi-a, pi-an-o
Pi-a, pi-an-o.

Dingle-dangle scarecrow

2+
years

This is one of the best action songs for young children. They can get into the character of the scarecrow and they love the contrasting actions of being small and then jumping up and pretending to be the scarecrow.

When all the cows were sleeping and the sun had gone to bed
    Action 1: Curl up, head tucked in.
Up jumped a scarecrow and this is what he said:
    Action 2: Jump up. Body should be limp with a hanging head.
"I'm a dingle-dangle scarecrow with a flippy-floppy hat
    Action 3: Make a rocking motion from foot to foot, with a floppy body and nodding head.
I can shake my hands like this
    Action 4: Shake hands limply.
And shake my feet like that."
    Action 5: Shake feet limply.

Tip box   ■ See page 68 to make your own scarecrow.

Other activities to try

Read a story that includes a scarecrow.
- - - - - - - - - - - - - - - - - - - -
Find some old clothes so your child can dress up as a scarecrow.

When all the hens were roosting and the moon behind the cloud
    Action 1: Curl up, head tucked in.
Up jumped the scarecrow and shouted very loud:
    Action 2: Jump up. Body should be limp with a hanging head.
"I'm a dingle-dangle scarecrow with a flippy-floppy hat
    Action 3: Make a rocking motion from foot to foot, with a floppy body and nodding head.
I can shake my hands like this
    Action 4: Shake hands limply.
And shake my feet like that."
    Action 5: Shake feet limply.

Traffic lights game

2+ years

From an early age children are very much drawn to the changing colors and patterns of traffic lights. This game is fun to play, but it also reinforces the meaning of each traffic light signal. Again, it's a stress-free game because no resources are required, you just need at least three children.

1 Ask the children to find a space.

2 Tell them they are going to play the Traffic Lights Game.

3 Remind them of what each color represents. Red = Stop. Yellow = Get ready to stop. Green = Go.

4 Tell the children that the traffic lights are currently on red, so they should be still.

5 Tell them that the lights are about to turn to green so they should get ready to go.

You will need

- Large indoor or outdoor space

Tip box ■ For younger children who are not as familiar with the names of colors, try holding up pieces of red, yellow, or green card as you say each color aloud.

6 Tell them that the lights have now turned green, so they should go.

7 When they are new to the game, start them off just walking forward when you say green. To make the game more challenging for older children, once they are confident of your instructions on each color, you could choose a different action for them, such as walking on their tiptoes, taking giant steps, or running in zigzags.

8 Go back to yellow to get them to slow down, and then to red.

9 Go through the sequence again and again with different actions on the green light signal.

Other activity to try

There are endless action possibilities for this game. You could use animal actions, such as "walk like a penguin" or transport actions, such as "ride a bike."

This is a favorite action song: "If You're Happy and You Know It." Children love to sing it as it's a real expression of their joy and reminds them of all the actions they are capable of.

If you're happy and you know it clap your hands. [Clap, clap]
If you're happy and you know it clap your hands. [Clap, clap]
If you're happy and you know it
and you really want to show it . . .
If you're happy and you know it clap your hands. [Clap, clap]

If you're happy and you know it stamp your feet. [Stamp, stamp]
 If you're happy and you know it stamp your feet. [Stamp, stamp]
If you're happy and you know it
and you really want to show it . . .
If you're happy and you know it stamp your feet. [Stamp, stamp]

Continue the verses with other actions, such as:
• Jump up and down.
• Turn around.
• Stretch up high.
• March on the spot.
• Show a smile.

Traditionally the song always ends with the following verse:

If you're happy and you know it shout,
*   "We are!" ["We are!"]*
If you're happy and you know it shout,
*   "We are!" ["We are!"]*
If you're happy and you know it
and you really want to show it . . .
If you're happy and you know it shout,
*   "We are!" ["We are!"]*

Try using the tune of this song to help your child to learn about the different parts of his body. You can do the actions of the song so that your child copies you.

Put your finger on your finger on your finger.
Put your finger on your finger on your finger.
Put your finger on your nose.
Turn around and touch your toes.
Put your finger on your finger on your finger.

Put your finger on your head on your head.
Put your finger on your head on your head.
Put your finger on your nose.
Turn around and touch your toes.
Put your finger on your head on your head.

Continue going through different body parts, repeating the nose and toes section. You might start at the head and work your way down.

Role-play

A role-play corner with dressing-up clothes is irresistible for young children. These are some tried-and-true role-play setups that you can create at home. When your children's new friends come over, these games are a great friendship maker. All you need to do is assemble the props and give them some help getting started, then you can leave them to create their own role-play.

Supermarket

1 With your props assembled, tell one child that he must be the customer, while the other will be in charge of the cash register and money. Tell them they can swap roles afterward so they get a chance to play both roles.

You will need

- Play food or empty containers of real food
- Toy cash register
- Play money
- Baskets or bags

Tip box

■ The secret of a successful role-play setup is to change the objects or dressing-up clothes in it every few weeks to keep your child stimulated by it.

■ Younger children would also enjoy playing simple versions of these games, although they may need more guidance from you in playing make-believe.

Shoe shop

1 It doesn't matter if your collection of shoes are adult-sized and won't fit the children, they will still love this role-play, and the fun of dressing up with "grown-up" shoes. Again, make sure the children swap roles so that they each get to play both roles.

- As many shoes of any size that you can lay your hands on
- Toy cash register
- Play money
- Baskets or bags

Builders

1 The children can try building their own little structures. You could start them off by asking them to build things for you, beginning with something simple, such as a small wall with their building blocks.

- Hard hats
- Toy tool kit or tool belt
- Toy telephone
- Pad and paper
- Checked shirt and overalls
- Building blocks

Police station

1 This is a good opportunity to start underlining the concept of right and wrong and discussing what sort of things the children think might be wrong or a crime.

You will need

- Toy police helmets
- Desk area with toy telephone, paper, and pens

Vet clinic

1 Show the children how to wrap bandages around the limbs of their soft toys. You will probably have to help them with this at first. Make sure they only use toys for this game and don't enlist any family pets as their patients.

You will need

- Toy vet's bag (or doctor's bag)
- Desk area with toy telephone, paper and pens
- Leaflets from your local vet's reception area
- Pair of scales
- Animal soft toys (which could be in lidless shoe boxes to create a recovery area—some could have bandages on)
- White coat or apron
- Some boxes to act as animal carriers to bring in and collect the animals

Medical center

1 Show your child how you can make a simple sling for a broken arm. You can use dolls or teddy bears as the patients for this role-play, or one of the children could be the patient.

Tea party

1 Assemble the guests around a low table, or even outside for a picnic-style tea party. You can fill up the teapot with some orange juice for your child to pour out for everyone.

Teddy bear parachute

1+
years

All children adore this activity. It is a fun way of including their favorite stuffed toy in their games. It consists of making a parachute for their teddy bear and then having a race to see whose parachute keeps their teddy bear floating down for the longest. It works best with several children.

You will need

- String
- Scissors
- Man-sized handkerchief for each teddy
- Teddy bear per child

1 Start by making the parachutes. Cut four pieces of string, about 16 inches (40 cm) in length, for each teddy bear.

Tip box ■ The children could decorate the parachutes with fabric paint or pens.

2 Attach one end of each of the four strings to each corner of the handkerchief. The children will need help tying the string.

3 Tie the other end of the strings to the arms of the teddy bear, to make a harness.

4 Let the children test out their teddy bear parachute, so they get the idea of the game before the race.

5 When all the parachutes are completed, line up the children.

6 Ask them to hold up their teddy bears as high as they can.

7 Tell the children that after a count of three, they will release the teddies and the last teddy bear to touch the ground is the winner.

Other activity to try

The children could hold a blanket around the edges, put the teddy bears in the center, and toss them up.

The pirate game

3+ years

This game works well with children from the ages of two to ten and they always become totally absorbed in the imaginary pirate world that has been created. Be prepared to enter into that world and to lead them through alligator swamps, rickety rope bridges, and haunted castles to eventually find the treasure, and then back home again. You can have as few or as many props as you want, and it won't affect your child's enjoyment of the game. The game is best played with two or more children.

1 Set up your tent or sleeping bags as an island camp at one end of the space. If you don't have these props, drape blankets over chairs to make a den. Put the backpacks, flashlights, and shovels at the other end of the space and hide the treasure map in your pocket.

2 Tell the children that they are going on an adventure called the "pirate adventure," that begins at Grandma and Grandpa's house. Ask the children to lie down in the center of the space as if asleep.

3 Tell them that it's a lovely sunny morning and very shortly the alarm will ring and they will need to get

You will need

- Large indoor or outdoor space
- Selection of other props such as backpacks, flashlights, blankets or sleeping bags, a tent, a child-sized shovel
- Treasure map (see page 74 for how to make one)
- If you can rope in another adult or older sibling to help, even better

Tip box ■ Be prepared for the children to get very excited when playing this game. Make sure you have some quieter moments within the game.

dressed as if they were
going to the beach.
Make the sound of an
alarm clock, and the
children will get up
and pretend to get
dressed. Then ask them
to go to the bathroom
and pretend to wash
their faces.

4 Remind them that as they
are going to the beach, they will need to put on
a sun hat and sunscreen. Get them to pretend to do
these things.

5 Become Grandma and call them down to breakfast.
Lots of miming of eating cereals and toast. Grandma
tells them after breakfast they should go up to the attic
to bring down some of Grandpa's books.

6 Climb the attic stairs and there, among the books, is the
treasure map. Now you can produce the treasure map.
Agree with the children that they are going to go and
find the treasure, and that they will get to the island
using Grandpa's rowboat.

7 Send each child off to get things for the adventure—the backpacks, flashlights, shovels, and some imaginary things, like food, water, rope, and binoculars.

8 Creep down the stairs, out of the front door, down the windy cliff path to the beach, and into the rowboat. Look through your imaginary binoculars and discover that there is a band of pirates heading for the island who are also after the treasure, so you have to row very quickly.

9 At the island, set up camp. Gather firewood and make a fire. Toast food over the fire on long sticks.

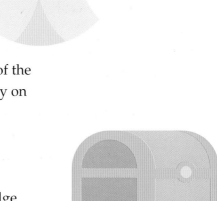

10 Go to sleep, but sleep is interrupted by the sound of the pirates. In whispers, clear the camp and creep away on hands and knees.

11 Check the map and discover that you have to go through the alligator swamp. On arriving, you discover the bridge is broken. Make your own bridge with the rope you have brought with you. Put a hook in the end and throw it across.

12 Get the children to stand in a line and swing each one across to the other side of the bank. If you have another adult, get them to stand a little way from you to receive the child. When all the children are across, check the map again to discover that the treasure is in the haunted castle.

13 The pirates are keeping watch over the castle so you have to swim the moat, throw a rope up to climb the castle walls, and balance along the battlements until you reach the castle turret where the treasure is hidden.

14 Check the map again. Count out with paces the place where the treasure is hidden.

15 The pirates are approaching. You have to dig very fast to find the treasure.

16 To escape the pirates you have to go very quickly. Repeat all the actions you have gone through but in reverse order. After returning to the campsite, go straight into the boat.

17 Having escaped the pirates, you arrive out of breath back at Grandma and Grandpa's house, where Grandma has made a delicious tea.

Other activities to try

Younger children may also enjoy playing a simple version of this game. Limit the length of the game and keep the actions simple so that they are able to follow what is happening.

You can extend or vary this game in any way you like to include completely new and exciting adventures and actions for the children to do, so they'll never tire of it. For example, perhaps they also need to rescue someone who has been trapped in the castle or kidnapped by the pirates. Or you could introduce songs into the game, such as "Row, row, row your boat" as you are pretending to row across to the island.

Language and stories

My philosophy has always been to show children not only the sheer pleasure that can be afforded by language but also how it can be used as a powerful tool to express their feelings and emotions. I would advise you to take every opportunity to enrich your child's life with stories, poetry, and songs. The activities in this chapter encompass every aspect of language development from clapping rhythm games to creating a pictorial storyboard.

Development timeline: 3 years plus

Once he reaches three years old, your child will have an ever-increasing roster of friends. The more time he spends with them, the more he will learn about cooperation and playing together. In play he will learn that the ability to share with others is important. If your child has siblings then he may have already had some experience of sharing or being asked to share, but if he is an only child it will be new to him and he may find it difficult to start with. Coupled with this, there will inevitably be conflict, and he will also learn how to negotiate, whether it's with his friends for another turn with the bricks or with his parents for an extra cookie.

Your child's sense of independence will now have been augmented by his increasing ability to dress and undress himself with simple items of clothing, although some parental input into his exact choices of clothes may still be required to

Timeline

cooperates more
with other children

increasingly able
to share

36 months

able to draw
recognizable
shapes

avoid unseasonal whims. He will now also be able to put his shoes on by himself, but if the shoes have laces they will have to be tied by someone else.

By this time, your child will be starting to have a better understanding of himself and his surroundings. As a result, he will be able to understand the difference between himself and younger children, but as yet unable to comprehend the difference between himself and older children. He will be able to say his age and will feel quite grown up by now, so he will take great pleasure in looking at photos of himself as a baby.

The activities in this chapter will help to develop your child's ever-increasing vocabulary as well as encouraging an interest in stories. You will also be able to prompt your child's memory of words, stories, and objects with activities like I Went to the Store and Bought . . . and Set Stories with Props, where he will begin to associate key objects and props with the stories he knows. Encouraging him to participate in activities such as Making Up Stories with Props and Storyboard will also develop his enthusiasm for making up and sharing his own stories with you.

capable of
dressing and
undressing self

increasingly
independent

capable of
putting on
shoes

My family and friends

Family and friends are very important to young children, not only in the social sense but also as a means of identifying themselves and their place in the world. This next activity will help your child to establish who her family members are and where they fit in, in relation to her.

1 Set out the photographs of just the immediate family, scissors, pencil, and marker.

2 Invite your child to come and join you.

3 Explain to her that she is going to make a house with all the members of the family in it.

4 Let her select one of the photographs.

5 In pencil, mark a circle around the photograph so that it will fit in one of the windows of the house.

6 If she is able, let her trace around the pencil circle with the marker.

You will need

- Photographs of members of your family and of your extended family
- Pair of child's scissors
- Pencil
- Marker
- House template (see page 158), you may need more than one
- Glue stick
- Some crayons, colored pencils, or felt-tip pens
- Large sheet of paper to stick the houses onto

Tip box ■ Remember to include photos of any pets you may have. ■ This could be an ongoing project done over a period of a week or two.

7 Start cutting around the circle and then, if she is able, let her complete it.

8 Repeat steps 4 to 7 with another photograph until all the immediate family photographs have been cut out.

9 Take the photocopy of the house and let your child select one of the photographs.

10 Explain to her that she needs to choose which window she would like to stick the photograph in.

11 Once selected, she needs to glue the back of the photo and stick it in the window.

12 Repeat the process until all the photographs have been stuck onto the house.

13 Under each window, write the name of the family member in the photograph.

14 Invite your child to color in the picture.

15 Take another photocopy of the house and repeat the above steps but this time use photographs of any grandparents.

16 The same can be done on a separate house for any other extended family members like aunts, uncles, cousins, and so on.

17 When all the houses are complete, you may like to stick them onto a large sheet of paper, with the immediate family house in the center and all the other houses around it.

18 Draw a connecting line with an arrow from an immediate family member to the related extended family member's house. On the line write, for example, "Grandma and Grandpa's house, we get there by car." As well as the word "car," draw a picture of a car.

19 Continue until all the family members' houses have been connected up.

20 At the top of the sheet of paper you may like to write "All my family."

Other activities to try

After having completed all your family, you could repeat the same activity, but this time your child could make separate houses to include all her friends.

- -

Draw an extra window if there are not enough, or you could create a garden around the house and put other family members there.

The clapping game

2+ years

This fun game requires no resources, just a pair of hands. It can be played with one child or as many children as you wish. While your child is having fun, subconsciously she is developing an awareness of the rhythms and patterns of speech.

1 Sit facing your child, or if there is more than one child, in a circle.

2 Start by saying the child's name out loud and as you do so, clap out the name according to the number of syllables. If there is more than one child, go through their names as well.

3 Clap out the names of family and friends.

4 Clap out their favorite animals or things your child likes to eat.

Tip box   ■ Instead of hands, you could use homemade instruments. See The Kitchen Band on page 92.

I went to the store and bought . . .

You may have played the game as a child where you have to remember a cumulative list of items bought on a supposed shopping trip. This is a simpler version for younger children. It's best played with two or more children.

1 Ask the children to sit in a circle.

2 Tell them that they are going to play a game called I Went to the Store and Bought . . .

3 Put the objects in the center of the circle.

4 Give the basket to the youngest child.

5 Let her choose an object from the selection.

6 When she has chosen, ask her to say, "I went to the store and bought . . ." followed by the name of the object she selected. Then she puts the object in the basket.

You will need

- Selection of child-friendly objects (each child should have 1 object to put in the basket)
- Medium-to-large basket
- Towel or cloth large enough to cover the basket

Tip box ■ If a child is having difficulty remembering, give her some hints, but stress to the other children not to give the answer away.

Other activity to try

As the children gain more confidence in remembering, you can increase the number of objects each child selects to put in the basket.

7 The basket is passed around to the next child, who selects another object to put in the basket.

8 When all the objects have been put in, cover the basket with the towel.

9 Ask each child in turn if they can remember what object they bought.

10 When all the children have been asked, uncover the basket so the children can see if they were correct.

Alphabet hunt

This is another version of hide and seek, only instead of children hiding, it is done with objects. Each object should have the same initial letter sound, so that your child becomes more familiar with the alphabet and the way the letters sound.

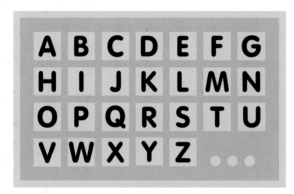

A B C D E F G
H I J K L M N
O P Q R S T U
V W X Y Z • • •

You will need

- 4 medium-to-small objects, each with the same initial letter sound (e.g., carrot, comb, and clip)

1 Show the objects to your child.

2 Check with your child that she is clear as to what the objects are.

3 Tell her that you are going to hide the objects.

4 Ask her to cover her eyes while you hide the objects.

5 Tell her when you are ready, and then ask her to find the objects.

6 If she is having difficulty finding one of the objects, you might need to give her a clue.

7 The game is over when all the objects have been found.

8 Recap the objects that have been found and the letter that they all start with.

Other activities to try

Once your child is confident finding the objects, you could increase the number of objects to be found.

When this game has been mastered, and as your child becomes more familiar with letters, instead of finding objects that all begin with the same letter, try going through the whole alphabet. Ask your child to find an object that begins with the letter "a," then the letter "b," and so on. Don't go through the whole alphabet at once; try four letters one day, and perhaps the next four letters the following day.

Tip box ■ If you are playing this with more than one child, ensure that there is one object for each child. Ask each child which object they would like to look for. Once they have found their object, they could help another child if needed.

Making up stories with props

In this game a prop acts as the starting point for a story of your child's own making. You could use literally anything, but listed below are some suggestions that work particularly well.

1 Tell your child she is going to make up a story.

2 Show her the prop that you have chosen for her.

3 For the adult shoes, you might like to suggest that they belong to a giant. Ask your child to describe the giant, where he or she lives, and what adventure does he/she go on.

You will need

- Selection of props such as a pair of adult shoes, a selection of hats, or a wrapped-up parcel with a sign saying "please open me"—inside there should be an object of your choice

Tip box

■ Children will need continuous promptings to help them develop the story. Ask questions such as: What happened next? Did they get back safely? Was she scared when she saw the lion?

■ You will need to act as a guide to bring the story to an end.

4 For the selection of hats, you might explain to your child that she is going to pretend that the hats belong to some other people. Ask her to describe them and why they wear the hats.

5 Children can't resist the appeal of unwrapping a parcel, so this one makes a great starting point for a story. Whatever you put in the parcel is going to determine the type of story you create. You might put a ring in the parcel, for example, and explain that the ring has special powers, and then ask your child to tell you what they might be and who owns the ring.

Set stories with props

3+
years

In this game you are using the props to tell a story with which the child or children are already familiar. They have to guess from the props set out before them which story it is, tell that story, and then act it out. Think of a favorite story and what props you could use to represent the story so that your child will instantly recognize and associate with it.

You will need

Props appropriate to the story— for example, for *Goldilocks and the Three Bears*:

- Large, medium, and small bowls
- 3 spoons
- Box of porridge oats

1 Lay out all of the props you have chosen in front of your child.

2 Ask her what story she knows that includes three bowls of porridge. You might need to point out the different sizes of the bowls to help her.

3 You could then ask why the story is called *Goldilocks and the Three Bears*. What does this little girl do?

4 Keep asking questions until your child has told all the main events in the story.

5 Get your child to use the props to act out the events of the story.

Other activity to try

You can play this activity with any number of children's stories. For example, for *Little Red Riding Hood* you would need props such as a red cape with a hood, or just a red-hooded sweater would work well, and a basket of goodies for her to take to Grandma. Ask your child what story includes a red cape. You could then ask why the story is called *Little Red Riding Hood*, what does this little girl do? Again, keep asking questions until she has told all the main events in the story.

Tip box ■ If you are doing this with several children, make sure you have chosen a story each of the children is familiar with.

Storyboard

3+
years

In this activity, you use pictures cut out from magazines to create a storyboard from which your child can make up his own story.

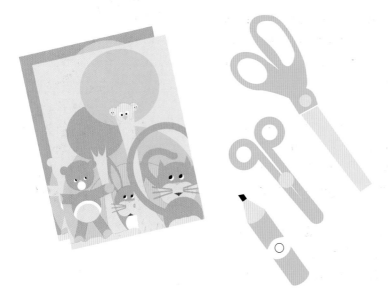

You will need

- Selection of old magazines
- Pair of child's scissors
- Adult scissors
- Black felt-tip pen
- Piece of card stock or paper
- Glue stick

1 Ask your child to cut out pictures that appeal to him from the magazines. To help him, tear out the page first and circle with the black felt-tip pen the picture he wishes to cut out.

Tip box ■ Don't worry if you can't use all the pictures in the story. They can be saved for another time.

2 Let him collect about ten pictures.

3 Ask him to spread out the pictures next to the paper.

4 Find among the pictures one of a person or an animal. If it is a picture of a person, prompt his imagination by asking him what name the person might have. If it is a picture of an animal, ask if the animal is a boy or a girl.

5 Ask him to glue the picture on the top left-hand side of the paper, and if you want to, write the name of the person or animal underneath. Tell him that you are going to make up a story about this person or animal.

6 Ask him to look at the other pictures and to tell you what happens next. You may need to make some suggestions to get him started. Does he go on vacation? Does she go shopping?

7 Continue until all the pictures have been used and glued down in a row across the paper. If you don't have enough space, make a second row.

8 Recap the story, picture by picture.

Out and about

Every day for a child is a day of discovery and learning. This does not mean as a parent that you have to bombard your child with new experiences. Children will derive the utmost pleasure from observing the tiniest insect or hearing the leaves being rustled by the wind. The key to helping your child discover the world around her is to allow her time to explore, investigate, and question. The activities in this final chapter will stimulate and engage your child's natural curiosity and expand her knowledge of the world she lives in.

Out and about

The outside world will become more and more familiar to your child as the years go by. Some children will have an earlier start than others depending on whether or not both of their parents work away from the family home. While exposure to external influences is vital for your child's education, it is always wise to ensure that she experiences a rich variety.

From birth the daily routine of your child should include a walk around the neighborhood. As she develops, she will be able to take in more and more of what she sees, and what goes on around her, on that daily walk. If you are lucky enough to have a park nearby, then a knowledge of the natural world can be introduced very early. Once she has started to take her first steps, your child can be taken out of her stroller and introduced to the trees and the birds, and as she grows, she can explore the outside world further.

When your child has learned a few words, your daily walk can be turned into a game and you can tell her all about the things she sees and hears, from the cars on the street to the bakery on the corner. Being able to then associate the things she has seen with the role-play games in this book will be a tremendous help. If you can organize a trip to a working farm, then your child can start to learn about all the different animals. To be able to see the process of milking a cow will be a fascinating experience for her.

Ultimately, whenever you are out with your child, wherever that might be, any amount of information you can pass on to her about what she can see and hear will be invaluable in her development.

This chapter gives you ideas of activities and games that will help your child learn about and interact with nature, as well as improving your child's understanding of the world around her.

Sticky the Squirrel

2+
years

This is a great game as it combines so many activities and skills. It begins with the character of Sticky the Squirrel. In a story about him, your child will learn about squirrels and their habitat. The game ends with a seek-and-find activity.

Before you start the story, you will need to cut out the template of Sticky, letting your child help you if he is able. Then ask your child to color in the picture and write at the top of the sheet "Sticky the Squirrel." Then you're ready to tell the story of how Stanley the Squirrel became sticky.

You will need

- Photocopy of the squirrel template (see page 159)
- Child's scissors
- Adult scissors
- Colored pencils, crayons, or felt-tip pens
- Garden or park
- Double-sided tape
- Assortment of natural objects, such as leaves or twigs

How Stanley the Squirrel Became Sticky

Once there was a squirrel called Stanley. He was a very inquisitive squirrel, who liked to go exploring all through the woods where he lived. Up high in treetops, down in deep hollows under piles of autumn leaves, there was no place that Stanley had not explored. One day on the soft breeze came a delicious, sweet smell. Stanley followed the smell and it led him to a beehive. The delicious smell was, of course, the honey. Now Stanley knew that bees sting, so he waited until the bees had flown away to collect some nectar. Then he raced into the hive to steal some of the delicious honeycomb. Away he ran with it, taking it to his favorite tree. Unfortunately Stanley was not a very tidy eater; in fact, he was rather messy. The more honey he ate, the more it spread all over his fur from the top of his head to the tip of his tail. Try as he might, he could not remove the honey from his fur. Everywhere he went all sorts of things stuck to him: leaves, twigs, and feathers. So since that day Stanley became known as Sticky.

Tip box

- Let your child make his own selection of things to stick on but remind him that they need to be small and light.
- Check that the outdoor area is free from prickly plants or any sharp objects, etc.
- This is a good opportunity to explain not to pick living things such as plants.
- If more than one child is playing the game, ensure that you make a photocopy for each child.

1 Take the drawing of the squirrel to your outside space.

2 Ask your child to rub his hand over the drawing. Explain that at the moment he's Stanley the Squirrel, but that you are going to turn him into Sticky the Squirrel.

3 Cut small pieces of double-sided tape and stick them onto the squirrel.

4 Peel off the top protective pieces and let your child feel a piece so he can see that Stanley is now Sticky.

5 Ask him to collect and stick on any objects that he thinks may have stuck to Sticky.

Other activity to try

If you don't have squirrels where you live, choose an animal that does inhabit your local area. You will have to draw your own picture of the animal for your child to use, however.

The alphabet game

This is a great game if you are stuck in traffic. It requires no resources and can be played with one or more children.

1. Start by telling your child that you are going to play the alphabet game.

2. Choose a topic list—for example, animal names.

3. Ask your child if he can think of an animal beginning with the letter "a."

4. Continue on to "b" and work your way as far through the alphabet as possible.

You will need

- Topic list (this can be anything you want, here are just a few suggestions: food names, animal names, items of clothing, colors)

Tip box   ■ If you have a group of children, let them take turns. If one gets stuck, the other children can help.

Colors in nature

Whatever the environment, children are drawn to color. This seek-and-find game introduces them to the variety of colors to be found in nature. At the same time, she will get to know the names of the colors and use visual discrimination to develop her color-matching abilities.

1 Start by gluing your colored squares onto the cardboard in two rows of three, evenly spaced across the cardboard.

2 Next to each colored square put a piece of double-sided tape of a similar size to the colored square. At this stage do not peel off the top protective strip of the tape.

3 Take the card with you when you go to your outdoor area and explain to your child that she is going to play a game of color matching.

You will need

- Glue stick
- 6 colored squares of paper approximately 1½ by 1½ inches (4 by 4 cm) in a variety of colors to match the outdoor space you have chosen (e.g., browns, reds, oranges, greens)
- Cardboard or stiff paper approximately 12 by 8 inches (30 by 20 cm)
- Double-sided tape
- Scissors

Tip box

■ Emphasise and repeat the name of the color when she is looking for an object of the same color: "You need to find something red."

■ You might want to begin by finding three colors and then working up to six.

4 Focus in on one color and ask her to find that color in the plants or trees around her. Explain that it just needs to be a very small amount of that color so that she can stick it onto the cardboard when she finds it.

5 Give her the cardboard and help her to look for the first color. Start by deliberately choosing things with colors that don't match. Put the object next to the colored square of paper and say, "It's not the same." In this way she will come to understand that she needs to find an object the same color as the square.

6 When an object is found, show her how to peel off the top strip of tape and stick the object to the sticky tape.

7 When all the colors have been matched, let her know what a good job she has done in finding and matching the colors. Run through all the things that were found and their colors; for example, "We found a red leaf."

Other activities to try

As she gets more confident in finding, let her explore by herself and show you her finds.

This game can be repeated, making a new color board with colors to reflect a change in the season.

Textures in nature

This is a seek-and-find game during which your child can develop his sense of touch as he explores the variety of textures to be found outside in the yard or park.

You will need

- Yard or park
- Collection of natural objects with varied textures that your child can clearly distinguish between
- Small container

1 Begin by collecting a range of objects from the yard or park—such as leaves, small stones, bark, twigs, feathers, petals, and grasses—and put them in the container. On this occasion don't let your child help you, so it will be more of a surprise when he has to do the seeking.

2 Let your child select one of the objects in the container.

3 Tell him that he needs to find where in the yard the object came from.

4 Walk around the yard, comparing the texture of the object in his hand with the tree bark, the grass, and so on, so that he gets the idea that he needs to match up the object using his sense of touch.

5 When the correct match is found, let him place the object with the matching one.

Other activity to try

The beach is a fun place for your child to explore textures—from the different textures of the sand, to all the different types of rocks and shells.

Tip box   ■ Start with three objects, working up to six when the game is repeated.   ■ Make sure that the matching object is accessible, and if not, cheat a bit and place it so that he can get at it.

Nature collage

2+
years

Children love to create and this activity allows them to freely create a nature collage using the natural resources of whatever is at hand in a particular outdoor space. This activity is best suited to autumn, when there will be a greater variety of colors in the grasses, leaves, nuts, and seeds available.

1 Find a level piece of ground where the collage is going to be created. It can be as big or small as you wish.

2 Say to your child that she is going to make a collage using all the natural things around her.

3 Ask her to begin by collecting all the things around her that she thinks will look good in her collage.

4 Make a little pile of everything that has been collected next to where the collage is to be created.

You will need

- Outdoor space that has a good variety of natural objects such as leaves, twigs, bark, nuts, seeds, etc. (you won't need paper or glue, as this is a natural collage, and so is not permanent)

Tip box
■ You might want to work alongside your child, creating your own collage, as this will help her to get some ideas.

■ Check the area for prickly plants and point them out to your child.
■ Remind her that such things as berries are only for the birds.

5 When enough things have been collected, ask her to see if she can make a picture or pattern with them. Suggest different shapes or patterns, like circles, spirals, or zigzags.

6 Once the collage is complete, allow her to step back and admire her creation.

Other activity to try

When your child has completed this, you could collect together some of the objects she has used to take home, so that she can put a smaller scale collage onto paper as well.

Treasure trail

2+ years

Children love following a trail, especially if they know there's going to be treasure at the end. This game can be played with as many or as few children as you wish. It's also a great game for older siblings to join in. For those reluctant walkers, they will be so busy having fun following the trail they won't even realize all the exercise they're getting.

1 Choose your outdoor space. You could use a large yard, park, bushland, or woodland—whatever is available or nearby.

2 Set a trail using the chalk to mark the way with large arrows, or blobs of flour when there isn't a place for an arrow.

3 Your trail should take about thirty minutes walking time.

You will need

- Outdoor space
- Piece of chalk
- Small bag of flour
- Treasure (such as stickers, cookies, chocolate coins)

Tip box

■ When following the trail, don't let the children race too far ahead of you. Always keep them within your sight.

■ If you are in a large group, have little rest stops to allow everyone to catch up and also ensure everyone stays together.

■ Make sure all your chalk arrows and blobs of flour are clearly visible at a child's sight level.

4 Explain to the children that they are going to follow a
trail and that they need to look out for white arrows
and blobs of flour.

5 When they get to the end of the trail, reward them with
their treasure. This could be anything from a special
sticker to their favorite cookie or you could even hide
some chocolate coins.

Seek and find

2+ years

This is a great game to play when you are outside and have no resources to hand. It is best played with several children. Children love the competitive element of trying to find items before anyone else. This game also has the advantage that within a group it can be played individually, in pairs or, if you have a lot of children, in teams.

You will need

- Large outdoor space with plenty of collectible things, such as leaves, twigs, and stones

1 Decide what objects you are going to ask the children to collect. For example, three green leaves, two twigs, one feather.

2 Tell the children what they have to find.

3 Send the children off to start hunting.

4 When they start returning with some of their finds, make a separate pile for each child.

5 When they have found all their collectibles, ask them to sit next to their pile.

6 The game is over when all children have completed the task.

Other activity to try

As the children become more familiar with objects outside, you can start to make the game more challenging by asking for more specific objects; instead of asking them to find a flower, ask them to find a daisy (only choose simple flowers that they are familiar with, and that you can see are growing in an obvious place).

Tip box

■ For younger children, only give them one item to find at any one time. When the children return with the object, tell them the next one on the list. Don't ask them to find more than one or two items.

■ Give each child as much freedom as possible in finding the things for themselves, but you might need to step in to help.

I spy

I doubt there is any adult that has not played this game, and it continues to be a favorite with children everywhere. When you introduce the game, try saying "Let's put on our looking eyes," and mime circles around your eyes with your fingers, as though they are a pair of glasses. This will help the child or children focus on the game.

1 If your child is new to the game, you could start by placing a group of objects on a tray. The "spied" object must come from one of the objects on the tray. When your child understands the objective of the game, place the same objects around the room.

2 Once the game has been understood in this way, introduce the standard way of playing "I Spy." You will need to go first.

3 Explain that you are now "spying" something from the room in which you are in. Spy something easy to start with.

4 If she is having difficulty guessing, give some clues— the shape, the size, what it is made from, and so on.

Street spy

Here is another game on the theme of looking and observing. It also has the advantage of encouraging your child to walk that little bit faster—invaluable if you need to get home in a hurry. The idea is to ask your child to spy specific things while out and about. The possibilities are endless, which means you can also adapt the activity to the age of your child to make it easier for younger children, then harder as they grow older. Here are some suggestions.

1. Ask your child to guess what color the front door of the next house will be.

2. Ask him to find a door that is the same color as your own front door.

3. Ask him to find a car with a license plate containing the first letter in his name.

4. Ask him to count the number of red cars he can see.

Other activity to try

A good book to introduce when your child has learned how to play I Spy, is Janet and Alan Ahlberg's *Each Peach Pear Plum*. It encourages close observation and introduces rhyming words.

Tip box ■ Always have your child walk on the inside of you when walking down the street, especially when playing this game, as his attention is taken with objects rather than potential oncoming cars.

Make a sand castle

2+
years

The charm of the sandbox is indisputable. It's also a perfect forum for your child to engage with natural materials creatively on a large scale. They will be entranced by the texture and qualities of the sand and be encouraged to stretch their powers of coordination and building.

You will need

- Sandbox, or a trip to the beach
- Suitable scoop or shovel
- Trays, molds, or buckets
- Water
- Decorative objects (such as shells, leaves, pebbles, flags)

1 Sit with your child and explore the possibilities of the sand by scooping, patting, and digging.

2 As he gets bolder, show him how to fill a mold or bucket and let him try it himself.

3 Turn the containers out to form shapes in the sand. Try mixing with water to get a firmer mold and create new textures for him to play with.

4 Show your child how to start building walls to connect together all the mounds he has made and complete his castle.

5 You can decorate the finished result with any objects you can find, such as shells, leaves, pebbles, or even a small flag to plant in one of the castle's towers.

Other activity to try

When your castle is complete, you and your child can build a moat going around the castle. With the wet sand, show him how he can build a bridge across the water.

Tip box
- Beware of sand in the eyes, ears, and mouth. Keep a bottle of clean water and a soft cloth handy in case of accidents.
- If more than one child is playing, make sure no one starts throwing sand.
- If you're at the beach, keep an eye on the tides and on how far your child is exploring.

Picnic time

2+ years

Picnics are exciting for children and adults of all ages. Even just heading out into the yard can feel like an adventure and a break from routine. Involving your child in every stage of the picnic and including an element of learning into the fun will expand her enjoyment and develop her ideas about how and where food can be consumed, what it looks and feels like in its different forms, and so on.

1 Preparation is half the fun. Tell your child you're going for a picnic and let her help you. Pack it together, talking about the different foods and where you'll be eating them.

2 Find a place outside that is quiet and safe for your picnic. It doesn't have to be adventurous, the back yard is fine.

3 Spread out your blanket and make sure you and your child are well protected from the sun.

4 Lay out the food by group and get your child to move around and have some of each. For each food group,

You will need

- Blanket
- Sunshade or beach umbrella
- Picnic food, to include all the food groups, e.g., pasta, fruit, eggs, yogurt, vegetables, chocolate
- Drinks

Tip box ■ You can combine your picnic with any number of the other outdoor activities suggested in this chapter.

talk about the colors, flavors, and shapes she encounters. The point is not so much to learn about the food groups as to enjoy the enhanced smells and flavors that come from being outside.

5 Sing along with your child to the song "The Teddy Bear's Picnic." This is a good song to sing while you're preparing the picnic, to keep her interested, and when you're outside enjoying your picnic together. You could even take some of your child's teddy bears out on the picnic with you.

If you go down to the woods today
You're sure of a big surprise.
If you go down to the woods today
You'd better go in disguise.
For every bear that ever there was
Will gather there for certain, because
Today's the day the Teddy Bears
*   have their picnic.*

Where on Earth?

2½+ years

From the earliest age children have a special love of animals. This next activity builds on this and extends their knowledge with an introduction of animal habitats in the form of a sorting activity. As with The Animal Game (see page 85), this is an excellent activity as a follow-up from a trip to the zoo. Alternatively, you could read to your child stories about animals of different habitats.

You will need

- Assortment of animals from farm and jungle habitats
- Container big enough to hold the animals
- 2 sheets of colored paper or card stock, 1 green and 1 brown

Tip box ■ Always allow plenty of time for your child to choose which habitat the animal should go in. If she is really getting stuck you may like to give her a few clues.

1 Put the animals in the container and take to a low table or the floor.

2 Invite your child to place the two pieces of colored paper, side by side, above the container.

3 Explain to her that the brown sheet represents where all the farm animals live and the green sheet where all the jungle animals live, and she needs to sort the animals and put them in their correct habitat.

4 Let her choose an animal and decide if it needs to be put on the green or the brown paper.

5 Continue in this way until all of the animals have been sorted into the correct group.

6 She may wish to repeat this activity in which case put all the animals back into the container and start again.

Other activities to try

Once your child has mastered sorting the animals into two habitats, you can introduce a third. Use a blue sheet of paper to represent animals who live in the water and an assortment of animals who live in the water, including dolphins and whales. Set out the activity in the same way as before, but this time put out all three sheets of paper.

- -

When your child is confident in sorting all three sets of animals, you can increase this to four and then five. Use a sheet of yellow paper to represent animals who live in the desert and a sheet of white paper to represent animals who live in the polar regions.

- -

This activity could be followed by introducing maps and discussing where on a map you would find these habitats.

Template 1

Story gloves

Cut out the figures
to tell the story of
*Goldilocks and the
Three Bears*

Template 2

Counting gloves

Cut out the cupcakes
to make the
Counting Gloves

Template 3

Flying fish

Template 4

Treasure map

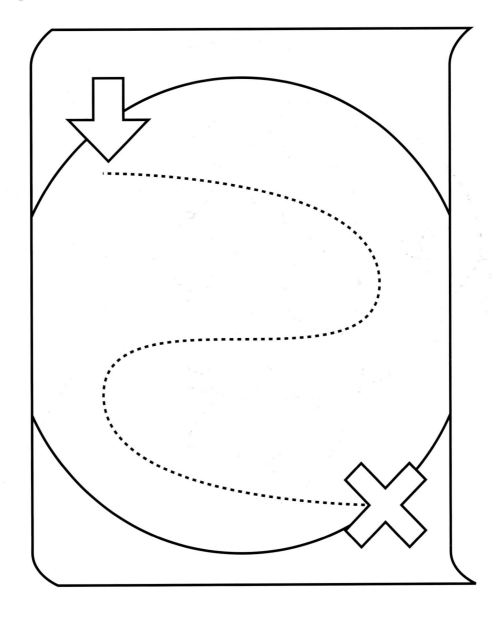

Template 5

My family and friends

Template 6

Sticky the Squirrel

Index